KUM INSIDE

"I'll Let You In"

KEITH "KCAM" CAMPBELL

Kum Inside
"I'll Let You In"

Copyright © 2025 Keith "Kcam" Campbell

kcamproductions@yahoo.com

Photos by: Jeron Thomas, jthom@jterreimaging.com

ISBN: 979-8-218-64965-4 (Paperback)

First printing edition 2025

TABLE OF CONTENTS

ACKNOWLEDGEMENTS

I would like to acknowledge every woman I had a sexual or intimate relationship with, because we all know sex is not only physical but we will get into that in the book. All of your sexual and intimate experiences helped put this book together.

Now sit back and let's take a hot and steamy look at some of these experiences that made this young man the sensual, erotic, lover he is today! ☻

WORDS OF ⚠ CAUTION

I advise you not to wear panties while reading this book because they are definitely going to get wet. I am not responsible for any damaged panties...❤

INTRODUCTION

L et's be honest with ourselves. Sex is one of the best ways to relieve stress, communicate, or just relax. When it's done right it can be addictive like a drug! In this book our author dives deep into the sexual journey of our character, from his youth until his adulthood. Vividly revisiting some of the most influential sexual experiences that molded him into the sexual beast he is today. We all have a need for sex but some of us just choose to suppress our desires and deprive our bodies of their natural needs. What better feeling than letting out a huge nutt of a massive explosion of squirting out of your vagina after a long day's work or after a stressful argument. In this book you will get to experience some of this from first hand events. Not only that but the author will take you on one of the best sexual journeys you will ever experience. So get in a private spot, clear your mind and prepare to start daydreaming through this steamy sexual rollercoaster. Just remember I'm not responsible for what you do during or after you read this book.

BORN TO BE WILD

From my earliest memories, I can remember that I loved women! Sexy beautiful well-built women, with that corporate slutty attitude. The kind of woman that has a nice ass, that makes any pair of jeans or a dress look seductive as hell. I mean if she puts on a sundress, with no panties you automatically get an erection. I remember being in grammar school sitting there looking at the female teachers, wondering if she had on panties. Sitting at my desk, trying to hold my dick down so no one would notice I had an erection. I don't know how many days I came home with a wet spot in my underwear and it wasn't from urine. Trust me, I wasn't a pervert, but I just loved women and the sexier the woman, the more I was turned on. Some men don't know the difference between sex appeal and good looks. Believe me, there is a difference. See, good looks are just a pretty face or a nice body. Those are things that a person could lose as they grow older but sex appeal is just something that stays with you forever. You know the way she twitches that ass or the way she bites her lips when she talks. Sex appeal can even be that sexy look she gives you when she looks you in your eyes.

There was this one teacher that had it all! I mean the way she smiled was sexy to me! That body could walk past me in the hallway and at my young age she would make my dick jump. It was never the girls my age that got me excited, because when I was growing up, the little girls were built like boys. I loved walking past the high school in the summer when the female track team was practicing. Seeing those high school girls in those little shorts and sports bras, definitely did something for a grammar school boy. I never stood there and stared like a pervert but I definitely got some looks in as I walked by. I remember when I was around eleven or twelve years old, my mom and dad put us in day camp. There was a female counselor and believe me she was sexy as hell. One day when camp was almost over, she asked me to help clean up the gym. While we were putting up some equipment, she closed the door. It was just us there. Before I knew it, she grabbed my hand and rubbed it on her breast. I was scared and trembling because I had never felt breast before.

After that, she kissed me and put my hand down her pants. Now my penis was having a feeling I never felt before and damn, it felt good; even if I didn't know what was happening. Before I knew it, her shorts were down and my pants were down. I remember her touching my face and tears were running down, so she stopped and pulled my pants up. She asked me if I was okay and if I was going to tell anyone. I never told anyone, and I wasn't okay, even though I told her I was. For a long time, I had an issue with women being aggressive sexually. Also, I think this may have been the reason I was so turned on by the older, sexy teachers. Even though she was older and aggressive, something turned me on about the entire experience. I had never seen an older woman's sexy, naked ass or tits, nor

2

have I ever felt a wet hairy pussy. Believe me, after that summer, every time I thought about the incident, my dick got hard. No matter where I was or who I was around. That lady gave me a moment to remember!

My first two sexual experiences would be with older women but the second lady took it a little further. The second time was when we were playing hide and seek on our block. Everyone was hiding, but I hid under the porch by myself. Next thing I know, one of the high school girls ran under the porch where I was and this was going to be a game to remember. I could hear everyone running out of their hiding spots so I got ready to run from under the porch. At that time, she grabbed my arm, pulled me back and covered my mouth. She started unbuttoning my pants, then pulled my underwear down. Next thing I know; she was on her knees sucking away on my dick. For this to be my first real physical sexual experience, it felt damn good. I can't recall if I ejaculated or not, but I do know that this could not have been her first time giving oral sex. After that, I was always looking forward to playing hide and seek with her again, but unfortunately, she never played again.

Having these two experiences at such a young age definitely made me and my dick ready for some real pussy. Unfortunately, this would not happen for another few years. I would have other close experiences before then. My dick would not actually get wet from some pussy until my senior year of high school. Over the next few years, I would meet young ladies and do a lot of playing with pussy or getting my dick played with, but never getting it wet. But there was this one time, I met this young lady, while I was working at McDonalds. We would hang out at her house sometimes after work or after school. One day while we were hanging out, she showed me some naked pictures in a magazine. I didn't think anything of it, but something else was on her mind. It was cold outside so we both had dressed in layers of clothes. I was sitting on the floor watching television and she went to her room. She said that she wanted to show me something else. I'm thinking that she is going to come back with some more naked pictures, but to my surprise, she came back in those sexy ass little shorts. I must say, for sixteen, she was built for her age and that was rare back then.

She said her mom bought her those shorts and asked if I thought they were too tight. Of course, I said no because the way that my dick was jumping in my pants, I definitely wanted to keep looking at her in those shorts. Well, the next thing I know is she sat down next to me and put her leg on me, right between my legs. She looked at me because her leg was on my rock hard dick. I smiled, then she reached over to grab it. I grabbed her tits while palming that round yellow ass. We started kissing and she was squeezing my dick. It was throbbing so bad that it was about to jump out of my pants. She let me start pulling down those tight shorts, which she had no panties on. I guess she knew what she wanted when she came back with those shorts on. By the time she got those shorts off, with all the squeezing on my dick, I had a huge wet spot in my underwear. It was a done deal. No matter how much I tried to get my penis inside her, it wasn't working. I had ruined the moment by letting go in my underwear. The funny thing is she wasn't that bad because at least my finger got some pussy. Once again, so close but still no wet pussy on my dick. I use to wonder if you don't put your dick inside her pussy, does it really count as sex? At this point, it really didn't matter to me anymore because if I was definitely going to bust a nut.

This is where my wild side came from because I embraced that old saying "There's more than one way to skin a cat," or in my case, there's more than one way to bust a nut. Even if a girl is on her cycle.... This one young lady was on her cycle, but kept kissing on me and making my dick get hard as hell. At one point, I told her if you keep getting it up then you have to get it down. She looked me in my eyes and said, "You know I'm on my period." I told her, "Well stop getting me excited, thinking that I'm going to get some." That's when she told me to just suck on her tits, but what good was that going to do this throbbing dick in my pants? Well, I did keep sucking on those tits, but being the wild boy I was! I definitely was going to get a nut. I politely took her shirt off, laid her down and climbed on top of her.

Then I took my dick and put it between those nice perky tits and went to work. Before I knew it, she was moving her head from side to side, trying not to get a nutt on her face. It was at that point, I realized titty fucking can make you nut, just like being inside the pussy. I still didn't know which one felt better because I hadn't gotten my dick wet yet. Believe me, the wild side of me came up with so many ways to bust a nut without actually putting my dick inside some pussy. Did I mention that she went to a catholic school?

Let's just say that those church girls or rather some of those church girls love to have hands laid on them. Not only do they love to have hands laid on them, but some of them love to lay hands as well. Our first encounter there was no beating around the bush. That catholic school seater came off, those nice yellow tits popped out and it was on. She kissed me, put one of those tits in my mouth, then started jerking my dick, nice and slow. Before I knew it, she had my pants off, sucking away on my dick, while rubbing it in between her tits. OMG!!! She made me bust all over her tits. The wildest part about the entire experience was she took her panties off and wiped the nut off her tits.

5

DAMN!! I felt like I had just had sex with a porn star. My two encounters with her were the best of my youth, until I got my dick wet.

I was finally coming up to my senior year of high school and little did I know that this would be the encounter that my dick would get wet by some good pussy. I had been dating this young lady since my junior year and we were so into one another. Everything about her was sexy to me. Everything! I loved the way she walked, the way she spoke, her build, the way she dressed and more. There was nothing about her I didn't like. We came up with nicknames for one another. We went to different schools, but we always found a way to spend time together during the school year. When summer came, we were inseparable. We were both still virgin, as far as penetration. We've touched on one another, but we had never done anything sexually; no fingering, oral or hand jobs. I haven't even seen her tits or any other parts of her body naked. But all of that was about to change.

It was the morning of prom and we both were super excited. I could not wait to see her dressed up! I was so nervous because we had both talked about losing our virginities on this day. I picked her up and of course, she looked more beautiful than I expected. We went to the prom and danced the night away. It was the true Cinderella story. The only difference is she didn't run off and leave a glass slipper behind. At the end of the night, I took her home. We had planned on getting a hotel room, so we could both loose out virginity. The next day, we were supposed to meet some friends and go to Great America. On our way to Great America, we both decided that we would rather chill at my house. Faith would have it that everyone was at work.

We chilled and listened to music for a while. We danced a little and started kissing. We ended up on my bed. I can remember everything so clearly. It was the perfect summer day. We were laying on the bed kissing as the summer breeze came through the window. I took my shirt off and as I imagined, those tits were perfect. I started sucking them like a baby trying to get milk. Next I took those sexy shorts off and again, as I imagined, she had the perfect ass and her pussy looked perfect. It looked so perfect that I did something and had no clue what I was doing. I went down and ate her pussy. Honestly, I know if this wasn't her first time having her pussy eaten, she definitely knew I didn't know what I was doing. I was so excited because it was going to finally happen. Also, I hadn't busted a nutt prematurely.

I came from under the cover and tried to put my dick in her pussy. She politely grabbed my hand and said "wrong hole." DAMN! I felt embarrassed. She grabbed my dick, then said "I'll do it." As she tried to put it in, she moaned while saying it might be too big. Why did she say that? Now my ego was inflated. It took a minute, but it was finally in and I was getting some wet pussy. I stroked and she moaned, which turned me the fuck on. But as quickly as it started, it ended. Man I was on cloud nine. I had finally busted a nut from some wet pussy. From that point on, things would only get better with our sex life. We experienced so much together and my pussy eating got better, because she definitely wasn't against me practicing. We would go on and date for a few years after high school, but eventually go our separate ways after I joined the Marine Corps. I must say, I had a wild sex life as a youth.

A TOUCH
OF SENSATION

In everyone's life, there comes a time when we discover our **genitals.** As an infant, we touch it but it's just because we are becoming familiar with our own bodies. But as we get older, we find out that our dicks and vaginas are for pleasure. Now the thing about that is, it can be pleasured by others or we can pleasure ourselves. Whatever way we choose to get that pleasure; it definitely leaves you feeling good. That first experience of realizing that your dick or vagina is for pleasure is different with everyone. Just so we are all on the same page, we do know that when you pleasure yourself, it's called masturbation. So My first time masturbating was in grammar school. I must have been in six or seventh grade. I was in class and that sexy ass teacher was in front of the class, reading a book to us. My mind definitely wasn't on that damn book. My mind was on those nipples that were sticking out of her shirt and that split on the side of her dress. Either way, I had a hard dick under my desk and boy was I rubbing the hell out of it. I had never masturbated before, nor did I have a clue what it was, but I was about to find out.

Before I knew it, my dick started feeling funny and I felt something coming out. FUCK!! That felt so good! I had just masturbated for the first time. WOW! I was on to something. Now I realized how to pleasure myself when I see these sexy ass female teachers. Every time I had this one class, I masturbated. The teacher was so fucking sexy that I had a hard on just walking into her class. I'm so glad that she didn't make me come to the chalkboard. Every man or woman remembers those long showers when they were a teen, pleasuring themselves. Well, if you don't I definitely do. Man, I remember that was the first thing I did when I got in the shower. Taking the soap and getting my dick all soapy while the hot water ran down my back. Stroking away, trying to get that good feeling because you know at that age, all you know was that feeling. The worst thing I hated was when you were right there, about to bust that nutt, and someone knocked on the bathroom door. DAMN! Now you have to start all over again!

The good thing is being so young, it was extremely easy to start over because almost anything you think about makes you horny.

At that age, you could think about cartoon characters and get horny. You could think about Wilma Flintstone in that short dress and get horny. I can't tell you how many times I sat around on Saturdays, watching the Brady Bunch and get a hard on from Marsha Brady. Hey, don't judge me, but as a kid, or rather a teen, her and Thelma from Good Times totally made me horny. As I grew up, masturbation became a hobby. It was like playing basketball, baseball, or any other sport. I looked forward to doing it. Masturbating became so addictive that I would rush home from school so I could get in the bathroom and stroke my dick. It was so bad, that I even forgot about pussy. See, I didn't have to put all the energy into talking to a woman and possibly getting rejected or she gets you rock hard and doesn't give you that wet pussy. All I had to do was get that Vaseline, then my hand would do the rest.

My hand never let me down or said no. I was always satisfied; we had a good relationship.

When I got older, I realized that masturbating could be a good thing, but we all know that too much of anything could be bad. If you don't know that if a man or woman masturbates too much, your penis or vagina can become desensitized to the real thing. Trust me, I know personally from a male and female perspective. The medical tern for men is death grip. It's when you attempt to get some wet pussy, the grip is not tight enough to keep you erect. This would happen to me several times as a teen and as an adult. As an adult, I was in a relationship with this young lady and she always played the pussy game. All guys know what the pussy game is! Whenever she's mad or doesn't get her way, she denies you the pussy. Like I told you, those games didn't work with me because me and my hand had a great relationship. She would play those games and wonder why I wasn't getting upset. Well, as soon as I left her, I would go home, put on a porno and masturbate.

To be honest, this became addictive! It was to the point that if she did offer me some pussy, I would've turned it down because my mind was on going home to masturbate. There was one time she wanted it so bad that she sucked my dick so long, her jaws started to hurt. It got a little bit hard but soon as she stopped and tried to put it in, my dick went right back down. She was so horny that she tried to give me a hand job to get an erection. It did get me hard because it was her hand gripping my dick, but as soon as she tried to climb on top of it. Down it went! I told her to keep going one time, when she was giving me a hand job, trying to get me hard. It was feeling so good, just like I was doing it. Before I knew it, I nutted all over her hands. She was pissed! Sitting there in her bed with some hot wet pussy, ready to get her a nut. I was laying there smiling because I busted a huge nut. Maybe this will teach her not to play the pussy games. This happened several more times in our relationship, until we both got tired and just let it go.

There was this one woman that I met who loved porn and masturbating, just like I did. When I say this woman showed me things! Trust me, her sex game was like nothing I ever experienced from younger to adulthood. Everything I did with her was like I was experiencing it for the very first time. She was about ten years older than me and I was in my early twenties. Talk about the perfect body, sex appeal, personality, and she was financially set. This was the kind of woman you marry right away before she gets away. Unfortunately, all she wanted was sex and for me to respect her. She had been married and divorced. Her mindset was that she wanted to have fun because she got married as a teenager and missed out on a lot, dealing with her cheating husband. Hey, I was down with it because I wasn't trying to be a step dad to a teenager.

Let me tell you about our first sexual encounter. It will know you off your feet. She called me in the middle of the day, to see if I had any plans. Of course I said no because I definitely wanted to hang out with her sexy ass. I drove to her house and when she opened the door, she gave me one of the most exotic kisses I ever had. Her tongue was all in my mouth! She sucked my tongue and then bit on my ear. That woman kissed me so good, while palming my ass! When she finished kissing me, she had my gum in her mouth. All I was thinking was "What the Fuck Just Happened!" When she turned and walked away, I could tell that she didn't have any panties on under that sundress. With her sexy ass voice, she politely said to me to take a seat in the front room, while she got us something to drink. As she walked back with the drinks, I noticed she didn't have on a bra. Those nipples were sticking out like head-lights. We sat there talking about how she missed out on things growing up, but she doesn't regret it because she has her son.

Next thing I know is she grabbed my drink out of my hands and sat it on the table. Once again, she started kiss-ing the shit out of me! She stopped kissing me, then stood in front of me, pulled up her dress and started fingering herself. The next thing she did blew my fucking mind! She so gently stuck her fingers in my mouth and told me to suck all of her pussy juices off her fingers. She did this two or three times, saying so seductively, "I want you to taste all of my juices." That sundress came off, she stepped up on the couch, over me, and grabbed my head and put it between her legs. This lady was riding my face like she was riding a dick. My face was soaked with pussy juice. The freaky shit was she licked the pussy juice off my face. This woman started sucking my dick, which was nothing new to me, but I told you everything she did was like the first time. She swallowed my whole dick down to my balls and did not gag. When she got ready to ride me, it went down because, remember, it was just me and my hand for a minute. This was not a problem for her, it's like she knew exactly what to do. She started giving me a hand job which again, wasn't anything new. But before I knew it, she was riding the shit out of me while stroking my dick.

Can you say multi-talented! I busted a huge nut inside of her. That scared the shit out of me because I wasn't ready for a baby. She would eventually tell me that she couldn't have any more kids. That woman fucked my brains out the first time I went to her house. Believe me, it wouldn't be the last! If you don't know about using sex toys with your partner, then you are missing out on some freaky action. I can't count the number of times she used her dildo and wanted me to watch. It was a turn on to her and she knew it was a turn on for me to watch her moan. Over the next few years, I learned so much from her. I would even learn how to keep my penis hard when I had masturbated too much. Me and this woman did some wild things together, but some of our best sex was when we watched porn together.

We would fuck for hours when we watched porn together.

After a while, we both decided to go our separate ways. Not that we weren't having fun but she was moving out of state with her job. She wanted to hook up one more time before we officially called it quits. I agreed and went over to her house. As usual she was ready, looking sexier than ever, but Being a little freakier. While she was doing things to me, she kept whispering in my ear "you will never forget me. I hope you're ready for your surprise." We must have done it about three or four times and each time, she got freakier. I was about to get up and go take a shower, when she turned on the lights, then said "Surprise." Her fine ass friend had been sitting in the corner of the bedroom, naked with a dildo, masturbating and watching. I honestly didn't think that was the entire surprise. I went to take a shower, then came back to get dressed. When I came into the bedroom, they were in the bed getting freakier than we had. They saw me looking and just smiled. I grabbed my clothes, got dressed and politely locked the door. I think the real surprise she wanted me to know was that she was bisexual. That might have been her next step for me, but we will never know.

After that experience, I never saw or heard from her again. Those experiences that I had with her would increase my sex life tremendously over the next few years.

I guess you could say, her sex was like a drug because I was always looking for that same high or something better each time I had sex. The things that she taught me got me popular with the girls my age and I was able to utilize those skills with them. Sometimes, this would cause a problem because none of them were as experienced as she was. So they would get all caught up in their emotions. This one young lady I met was a virgin. We both were in our mid-twenties, but I had a lot more experience sexually. I should have walked away from her before this even began. Just meeting her was a bad idea. This was a buddy of mine, his girlfriend's cousin. For a long time, I was into light skinned women. She was light skinned with long hair and thick. I mean she wasn't fat, but if she didn't push back from her plate, she would be fat.

My buddy asked me to go out with her because she was new in town and her cousin didn't want her just going out with anyone. I didn't mind but like I said in the beginning, I love sexy women. I always have and always will. She was definitely sexy and knowing myself, I was going to convince her to let me be her first. Well, we hung out for a few months and like I said, I convinced her to let me be her first.

Let's just say, what I did to her when we hooked up sexually for the first time, wasn't amateur. I went straight porn star, no limitations. I kissed her passionately! I fingered her, then made her taste herself. And it didn't stop there. I ate her pussy so good, it was like sucking the meat out of a neck bone. I shoved all of my dick in her mouth, but of course, she gagged. I fucked here three long hard erotic times and each time, I nutted all over her. To top it off, I even made her masturbate in front of me. I went all out.

This went on for some months before I would try to end it. Ending it wouldn't be so easy and it would almost cost me and my buddy our friendship. It would take her cousin threatening to call the police on her before she would leave me alone. I know that good wet juicy pussy is great, but sometimes, the headache that comes along with it makes me always resort to masturbating.

LOOSE CANNON

As I grew up with all the compliments I was getting on hav-ing a big dick and knowing how to use it, I became a loose cannon! I mean I was getting so much pussy, I felt like a celebrity. Now there was a time that I did get with a ce-lebrity. Well, she wasn't famous then, but she definitely is now. Anyway, that's a story I won't kiss and tell. Now there are several other stories that I will tell and they will know your socks off. Like the time I was dating this young lady and her father's girlfriend decided to mess around with me behind their backs. Talking about low down! She was be-yond low down, but that pussy was on point. I don't know what it was that attracted her to me, but she wasn't hesi-tant to approach me. This woman was short, pettily built, extremely attractive, and very well groomed. I mean she kept her hair, nails and feet done.

If I didn't say it, that is a major turn on for me. I love a woman who is well groomed. From the top of her head to the bottom of her feet. Being that freaky man that I am, there's no telling what I may do when we are having sex. You may catch me sucking your fingers, a toe in my mouth, sucking all your pussy juices, or getting even freakier. The more well-groomed and sexier you are, the more I lose control and don't hold back. Believe me, she had it all! I mean, everything and then some! I can still remember how she would always give me compliments on how I treated her boyfriend's daughter. She would make comments like "I wish her dad treated me like that" or tell the young lady I was dating that she better put it on me. I guess that was her way of letting me know on the sly that she was interested in me. I never picked up on the signs because she was older and with my lady's dad. Plus, who would be threatened low down to do something so close to home.

Come to think about it, she did have a little wild edge to her behavior. There were times when I would spend the night, she would be having sec and be extra loud. The next morning, if I were in the kitchen by myself, she would comment about it. She would say things like, sorry if you heard me last night, but I get carried away when I have sex. She might even tell me how she turns into an animal when she has sex. Thinking about it, I feel she was testing me to see if I would tell my lady anything before she made a move on me. I never said anything so I guess that gave her the okay. Now she was taking things a step further. Like bending over with her robe on so I could see that freshly shaved pussy or letting it come open in the front when I could see those nice round tits. Listen, I was in my late twenties, so I was totally naïve to it. Plus, who would think that the lady's father's girlfriend would be trying to give me some pussy.

A fifty something well established, sexy ass woman would want to give me some pussy. It must have been true, because she gave me some pussy several times! This woman fucked me and bought me things like I was her man. When she first made her move on me, I must say, she was smooth as hell with it. I was working at a clothing store and she came in asking me to help her find something for her guy.

We looked around while laughing and joking. I tried on a couple of shirts for her because he was close to my size. She eventually bought two shirts, then asked if she could take me to lunch as a thank you. I politely said yes and she took me to lunch. While we were at lunch, she asked me about my relationship and if I was happy. She even asked me if my lady had any of her father's traits of being selfish. I told her not really for the most part, we got along well.

She went on to tell me how he cheats and is extremely selfish with his money. How she is always doing things for him, but he never appreciates it. Next thing I know, she said' I wish he were more like you." Then she told me how she would date a younger guy like me if I were single. My only response was a smile. We continued eating and at some point, I felt her foot between my legs. I don't know how she got her shoe off but she was caressing my dick with her foot. I looked at her and she had this look in her eyes like, you know what I want, it's your move now. This was an awkward position but she knew I was interested because I didn't push her foot off my hard dick.

At one point, I put my hand down there and rubbed her foot more firmly against my dick. After a minute of that, she drove me back to work and asked when we would have lunch again. My response was whenever! The next day, she called the store and said she was outside. I took my lunch break and we weren't going to a restaurant this time. WE drove back to their house and let's just say, she had no clue that I was well experienced. I put it on her so freaky and hard, it was the first time I made a woman squirt. It definitely wouldn't be the last time because every time I got a hold of her little sexy ass, it was splash waterfalls! I would leave those legs shaking and I told y'all I was a loose cannon! I kept a box of magnum extra-large lubricated condoms. I was fucking her so good that she started taking risk, like asking me to fuck her in the house after everyone went to sleep.

I know it was a risk, but I did do it a couple of times. One time her guy worked overnight and I was asleep with my lady. She must have gotten horny in the middle of the night, so she texted me. "Come to the laundry room." My lady was totally knocked out! She had gone out celebrating her friend's birthday, so she was wasted. When I got down to the laundry room, she was standing there naked. I turned her around and bent her over and gave her oral sex like crazy from the back. She squirted all over the floor! I slammed my dick in and went to work. Good thing my lady was sleeping hard because I was trying to make her moan loud. I was killing her pussy in that laundry room. She must have squirted at least four times! It felt like she couldn't turn the water works off. That shit was so good, I had to pat myself on the back.

The funny thing is that the next morning, my lady made a comment to me. She told me that her father's girlfriend was so loud that she was going to say something to her. All I did was smile on the inside. She eventually broke up with the father due to his cheating. We didn't continue seeing one another after they broke up, I guess we both knew it was best to let it go. When I say I was a loose cannon, that's exactly what I was!

Back then, in my late twenties and early thirties, strippers were very popular. I messed around with a female stripper and dammit we had a lot of fun. Every time we had sex, it was off the charts. Not to count the numerous times she let me have sex with her friend while she watched. I have never met anyone freakier than her. I watched her fuck one of her friends with a strap-on. It was so hot watching her fuck another woman. One year, I had a birthday party, so I hired her and some of her friends to dance. Me

20

and about fifteen of my guys got a room and were ready for a good time. I had no idea she had a surprise for me. The party was going great. Every guy was getting a lap dance or getting pleasured in some way. Well, here comes the surprise. They put a chair in the middle of the floor, then told everyone to gather around. I was led to the chair by two of her girls. The music started and they started dancing all over me. One even gave me oral sex.

They blind folded me and I could hear them walk away. The music started again, but this time, I could tell it was only one girl. She was dancing on me, the guys were cheering, then she untied my hands, rubbing them all over her ass. I could tell she was completely naked because I was playing with the titties also. At some point, she stated giving me oral sex, while putting a condom on me. She got on top of me and started riding the shit out of my dick. She took the blind-fold off and it was her. Let me just say we put on a show right in front of all of my guys. They were cheering as she moaned loudly because you know I went wild to show off for my guys. Trust me, no one was disappointed with that show. She and I would become really good friends throughout the years, even when she stopped dancing. Outside all of that, we developed a solid friendship that we still continue today.

Let's take a trip down the road of those women who think they are so much better than anyone. The ones who look so good, have all of their shit together and always say they don't need a man. I would love to fuck these women, just to knock them off their pedestal. I knocked a couple of them off over the years, but it's this one that I had to bring her down. Not only did I want to bring her down, she was so arrogant, I wanted to literally break her. That's exactly what I did. She trash talked me and talked about how good her pussy was. Talked about how she only needs a man for

21

dick and how she dismisses them at will. Believe me from looking at her, I believed every word she said. That woman was fine beyond belief. I looked like someone carved her body out because it was so perfect. I can't think of one flaw this woman had besides her arrogant attitude. Being the man I was, this was a challenge for me and I was definitely up for it. See, complimenting her wasn't going to do it. She was used to that. Taking her out or spending money wasn't going to do it. She was definitely used to men doing that.

I would have to do the total opposite of everything she was used to. See, she was a friend of a female I always hung out with. So when we hung out and all the guys were complimenting her and all over her, I was laying back, not paying her any attention. When we would all meet up at the gym, no matter how great she looked in those spandex with her fat pussy print showing, I wouldn't say anything. So one day, she and I showed up at the theater together, while we were leaving, she asked where our other friend was. I told her I didn't know but I'm about to go have lunch. She asked where, because she was hungry. This was an opportunity for me to set my plan in motion. I told her you're too high class to eat where I'm going. Of course, trying to hold to her status, she invited me to go eat with her.

After we ate, I told her this is on you because you invited me out to eat. She paid with no problem and then asked when I be at the gym again. She gave me her phone number and told me to text her when I was going to be there. My plan was falling into place. I realized that she will spend money on a man, even if it was just lunch. Also, she offered me her number and I didn't have to ask. Even if it was just to work out, it doesn't matter. She opened the door for conversation. A week went by, but I never texted her, then we all saw each other at the gym. The first thing out her mouth when she saw me was, "damn, I was expecting a call." In my mind, I was like I know, that's why I didn't call. I politely told her I forgot. I knew that would get to her because a fine ass woman like her, a man in no way would forget to call her. She told me that I do owe her a lunch, so I invited them both to lunch after we worked out.

While at lunch, she made a sarcastic comment about how she took me on a lunch date by myself but she has to share her lunch date. Of course I picked up on the word date and how jealous she was because she wasn't getting all of the attention. So I invited her out on a date and she accepted. My plan was fully in place. I would take her out several times but most of them would be because she asked. I never made a pass at her or tried to kiss her. All I did was hold her hand or put my arm around her. Now I had her mind because with her attitude, she was probably wondering why I hadn't made a move. Little did she know, it was coming, but she was going to be the one to initiate it. It was her birthday so I took her out. We had a beautiful time. Nice dinner and some nice cocktails. I was dropping her off at her house and gave her a hug. Before I knew it, she kissed me. Not only once, but she kissed me a secondtime.

I don't know if it was the liquor but she invited me in. Can you say birthday sex? There was no way I was going to go crazy on this fine ass woman. I promptly began to make love to his fine ass woman. I sucked her toes, gave her oral, and palmed all that ass. Now this was the time when I complimented the shit out of her every time I thrust my dick in her. I must have done a great job because the bed was soaked and she was fast asleep. After that, we dated for a few years and let's just say that arrogant attitude disappeared. I got gifts all the time. Never had to pay for any outings and she always offered to give me money. My plan actually worked. I brought her down, but I developed

feelings for her. So I couldn't dog her out. I rode the relationship out until we both went our separate ways. She
does reach out to me sometimes, on Facebook, talking
about how she loves her husband.

IT'S A MIND THING

Do you actually know that most men and women don't realize that sex is more mental than physical? Sex is actually ninety percent mental and ten percent physical. What most people don't understand is that the mind controls the body. Once you have someone's mind, you can get their body to do whatever you want. My grand-father always said "Men will lose money chasing pussy, but you will gain pussy chasing money." He'd always say, "don't let the pussy control you, instead you control the pussy." The only way you can control the pussy is keep your mind focused on your business and put the pussy in its place. Otherwise, prioritize the pussy. Whenever you let a woman feel her pussy is a priority over everything else, then you have lost. She will never respect you because she knows she has control.

Once I learned this lesson, I never let a woman feel her pussy was top priority in my life. Pussy stopped being ranked in my top five priorities in life. It may come in my top ten, but not my top five. Now, I'm not saying that I can do without pussy, but I'm not going to neglect my top five priorities for it. I have seen men who can't prioritize a pussy or have dick control, lose everything. I've seen men lose their marriages, jobs, money, and sometimes lose their lives over pussy. Sometimes, it's okay to walk away or say no. I have turned down more pussy than the average man gets. If I fucked every piece of pussy thrown at me or fucked every woman I know, I would have never written three books or excelled in my career. There was so many times that I was talked about by women just because I wouldn't fuck them.

If You learn to prioritize pussy and have dick control, that will be a game changer in your relationship. If you're not in a relationship, it will be a game changer in your life. How many times do women think they're in control because they are the ones with the pussy and they know that's what we want? Well if you let her know that her pussy is not a top priority, trust me, it will change the entire game. For some reason, when women feel that their pussy is not a priority, they are more eager to give you some. I guess in their mind, they feel rejected and wonder if something is wrong with them. They start feeling inadequate or insecure, like why don't he want some of my pussy. By the time I got older, I realized that I could never be pussy whipped. I hadn't been pussy whipped since I was in my teens.

I realized it's not the pussy that gets me, but the woman the pussy is attached to, that makes me go crazy or fall in love. Having this mindset would allow me to maintain relationships with women even after we broke up. I could be friends with them because they knew how I prioritized pussy. They understood that once it was over, and I put them in a friend zone, I don't mix the two together. Don't get me wrong, I've had some friends with benefits, but to me, that's a little different than straight friends.

Having a friend with benefits, you both have to have a mutual agreement. So it's kind of like a relationship. Whatever the case may be, it's different than being straight friends. When I say it's a mind thing, that pertains to physical sex also.

How many times have you as a man had a woman look crazy at you because you nutted too fast?

Trust me, it has happened to every man at least once in his life. If this is happening to you, it's because you haven't figured out that physical sex can be a mind thing. When I say that, I mean a man has to train his dick to align with the thoughts in his mind, so he won't nut too fast. Now, his mind can't be focused on that nice piece of ass, jumping up and down on his dick, but he has to distract his mind from what's right in front of him. This is in no way easy to do. I was fortunate to have a woman, rather an older woman teaches this to me. I would never forget what she taught me because I used it several times, while having sex with women and I still use it today. See, it's hard to not nutt when a woman is sucking your soul out or that wet pussy is all over your dick.

We were both managers at a clothing store, so we would open the store together or sometimes close together. Either way, we would spend a lot of time in the store together alone. She would always brag on how fine she was and how not many could handle her pussy or oral sex. Being the cocky sex addict I was of course I always made my smart remarks on how I would wear her ass out. I knew we both were curious about the opportunity that had not presented itself yet. That was all about to change. We were supposed to have a corporate visit at all the stores, but there was a horrible snow storm. None of the employees came in due to our transportation. It was only us in this store and hardly anyone was in the mall. We sat around listening to music, talking and just putting new merchandise out. So with my freaky ass I had to bring attention to the clothing she was wearing.

This lady always dressed seductive! Everything she wore showed the perfect shape of her ass or it definitely showed her pussy print. I asked her why she always dresses seductively revealing her body parts. She answered with a remark, "because I know freaky ass me like you are going to look!" Then I called her a tease and she did not like that. That's when she did not like that. That's when she told me that I talk a lot about how I could wear her out, but all I was going to do is became another brother who she destroyed. Of course, I said talk is cheap. Man oh man, she closed and locked the store, then put the will return sign on the door. It was time to see what all the talk was about. We went in the back room, she lifted that shirt up, pulled off that thong and aggressively said, "What's Up!" Basically, she was saying, you talked all that shit, now here is the pussy so what you going to do?

Shit was an easy answer for me, standing there looking at those sexy brown/caramel legs in heels, right in front of me, with no panties on. My jogging pants came down so quickly. All I could think about was getting in between those legs. I laid her down and slid my dick in her super wet pussy. She held those legs open so wide, letting me put all this big dick in her. I was going to work, but before I knew it, work was over and she had a look on her face like, "Damn, That's It!" My dick was drenched from her wet pussy as I stood up. She laid with her legs wide open, probably hoping I would get back down there in between them. It was a wrap for me. I had nutted so hard, even if I wanted to get back up, I couldn't. I will never forget what she told me. That day because I had never heard this before. Especially not from a woman. She said we have to work on your dick control.

I had no clue what she was talking about until she explained it. She said your dick is too big and to go for you to be nutting so quick. She said any woman would want a lot of playtime with that dick. So the next few times we hooked up, there were going to be lessons on dick control. This woman would teach me how to have good hard pussy pleasing sex without nutting so fast. How to have sex after you have nutted. I'm not going to reveal what she taught me, but let's just say, I was a beast in bed after all of her lessons. This one particular time we hooked up before the store opened and she was in for a surprise. All those lessons she taught me, I was about to use them on her and add a few tricks of my own. As usual, she came in looking extra seductive. I think she was in the mood because we had talked on the phone all night and I had been off work for a few days. So she really was in the mood for some of this big black dick and I was ready to please her.

She had on a sundress and from the looks of it, she either had on a thong or no panties at all.

That ass was bouncing. We went in and locked the door behind us and headed to the back room. I smacked her on the ass just so she knew when we got back there, what was on my mind. This time, I was the aggressor. I grabbed her from behind and palmed both those tits., then started sucking on her neck. I didn't just raise that dress up, I took it all the way off and like I said, she didn't have any panties on. I bent her over on the desk and started licking that pussy from the back. Something we had never done before. I started fingering her, then turned her over on her back, so that pussy was looking right at me.

I kept sucking on that pussy and the more I sucked, the wetter she got, while moaning loudly. Now I was about to pull another trick out of my head. I so gently stuck my thumb in her ass. OMG!!! When I did that, she squirted so damn hard, it looked like I turned a water sprinkler on. I was doing all this and had not even taken my clothes off.

She started grabbing for my dick, asking me to put it in. I started taking off all of my clothes and I rammed it right in but not in her pussy. Her mouth. I made her suck on all that big dick, while I continued to play with her pussy. She laid on the desk with her legs wide open. While I was doing all this to her my mind was always on what I was going to do to her next. Busting a nut hadn't even crossed my mind. I took my dick out her mouth and slid it slowly into her wet pussy.

I fucked her with just the tip of my penis for at least a good ten minutes. Then out of nowhere, I pushed my big black dick all up into her stomach. I went so deep in her she couldn't help but let out a loud moan. I fucked her so long and hard in that backroom that we opened the store thirty minutes late. Good thing no employees were scheduled to come in but us. The funny thing is I used everything she taught me and I didn't even bust a nut. The only reason I stopped is because I know I had my name stamped on it. She was so worn out that when the first employee came in, she went home because she said she needed to rest. She was done! I was fucking that pussy anytime I wanted. I had her coming to the job on her days off, just to get some of this big black dick. I totally had her dickmatized. She was definitely sprung.

It would not be until I was transferred to another store that we would stop fucking. She would still try to give me the pussy but I was on the other woman. We did remain cool, until she finally left the company and we lost contact. When you truly learn dick control, you have to be careful with what women you get with because all of them can't handle it. Some can't even handle regular dick. So imagine if you have a big dick and you have dick control. You can't fuck every woman like that. Listen, most women's emotions are connected to their pussy. So if you put that dick control on them, you just might have problems on your hands. Trust me I know. There was this one young lady that I went against my usual routine and hooked up with her. First of all, she was younger with her. That was my mid-thirties and she was in her early twenties.

She was fresh out of college and living on her own for the first time. WE met one day, while we were both getting gas. She mentioned my gym shoes that I had on. I was always into Jordan and this particular pair had just come out. We heard small talks about the Jordan's, then talked about a few other things. She was way prettier, than sexy, so like I said, I was going against my routine. I loved sexy women more than good looks. She was fine as hell, but kind of on the goofy side. She had a nice athletic build, but nothing to brag about. I still don't know what made me really go after her. Maybe, I just wanted to do something different. Whatever the case, we started hanging out and yes, she eventually gave me the pussy. I fucked this fine ass goofy girls so long and hard, with dick control several times. That was not a good idea on my part. She might have been fine and goofy, but she was crazy.

Whoever said crazy pussy is good is one hundred percent correct. This fine ass goofy crazy girl could ride the shit out of a dick. I mean, she could ride it from the front, look at me or turn around so I could see her ass bounce. No matter what way she rode the shit out of my dick. I knew from the beginning that this wasn't going to be a long turn, because I don't get into younger women. Why did I put this dick on her so well, because she wasn't going to let go that easily. When I tried to end it between us, she was furious. She tried to fight me, threatened to kill me and tried to damage my car. It took about six months of her doing stupid shit before one of my female friends confronted her. I guess this embarrassed her or maybe scared her, but she stopped and moved on. From that point on, I stayed with my routine, dealing with older sexy mature women. Those who know what they want and how to conduct themselves.

TRAINING DAY

When most people think about training, they reference it to a household pet, like a dog. If you didn't know, people can be trained also. I have seen people break up in relationships or get divorced because that person is not satisfying them sexually. To me, this is not a reason to get divorced or leave a relationship. You don't even have to step outside your relationship, if the person is willing to be trained on how to please you. In my life, there would be times that I would be trained but, there would be several times that I would be the trainer. In both situations, it would be great because you get to do it over and over again, until you get it right. Especially if it's something you like. This one woman loved for me to finger her pussy. No matter if we were driving, in the movie theater or anywhere. She loved to be fingered.

When I first fingered her, she said that I was being too rough and it wasn't making her cum. So she took the time to show me exactly how she wanted to be fingered. One day, we were at her house, on the couch, getting freaky and I started fingering her. She pushed my hand away so quickly, saying stop. At that time, she laid back with her legs wide open and said watch. The way she was playing with her pussy was so erotic. All she kept saying was, "see how slow and gentle I'm rubbing my clit?" At one point, she told me to touch her pussy to see how wet it was getting. Then she started fingering herself. She would use one finger, then two fingers and go back to rubbing her clit. This lady was fucking the shit out of herself right in front of me. I didn't know whether or not to be jealous because I wasn't getting her off or just sit back and enjoy the lesson. Either way, I was super horny, just looking at the pussy.

After that day, she never complained about me not doing it right. I would finger her so good that my hand would be soaking wet when I finished. It even came to the point that I would love to finger her in public because she would have to change her panties. The ones she had on would be soaked from cumming so much. I think one of the best lessons or training that I had was when this woman showed me how to eat her pussy. Now I had been eating pussy for a while, but she said you're doing it for your pleasure and not focusing on the pleasure of the woman. Most men do it just to get the pussy wet, so they can stick their dick in easier, but have not fully satisfied the woman with his tongue. She went on to explain that if that woman's pussy is not soaked with all her juices by the time you finish, then you have some more pussy licking to do.

So many men think because she is wet down there, he did a good job, but in reality, most of the wetness is his own saliva. After she taught me how to eat her pussy, I could definitely tell the difference between my saliva and the sweet taste of her juices. Did I forget to mention that this lady was bisexual? I'm sure you can guess how she taught me how to eat her pussy. There were times she would have me watch her and her friend eat each other's pussy. Then there were times she would watch me eat her friend's pussy or her friend would watch me eat her pussy. Her friend would tell me to lick the clit but don't neglect licking in the hole. She would tell me to gently rub her clit. I got so good at eating her pussy, I could make her cum and squirt quickly. I could even make her friend cum just by watching me get her off.

Those two ladies help me understand that when pleasing a woman, it's important to make her cum even before you put your dick in. If you understand that, then putting the dick in is just the icing on the cake. All the fucking you do after that is just bonus nut for her. Like I told you earlier, sometimes I was trained but there were times I was the trainer. So many women think they can suck dick but they must remember every man is different. There are actually some men that don't like their dick sucked. At one point in my life, I was like that. I did not like my dick sucked or I guess it was never done correctly.

Honestly, I would rather put my dick in some hot wet pussy. Suck my dick after I've busted a big nut. Just take your time and lick all the nutt and pussy juice off my dick. If a woman chooses to suck my dick before sex or penetration. Then do it right.

That's the good thing about sex, training someone on how to pleasure you. Ever since I really started having sex, I was told that I had a big dick. I was dating this one woman and she always told me that I was too rough and if I controlled my big dick, I would pleasure her more. That night, she would show me exactly what she was talking about. We were in bed and had already had foreplay. I was about to put my dick in her pussy, but she grabbed it and just put the tip in. She was fucking the shit out of my tip, like it was my whole dick. Before I knew it, she was screaming loudly that she was cumin. She started putting more of my dick in, little by little. Then she moved her hand, put her legs all the way back and grabbed my ass. She kept screaming,

"Fuck me hard!" And I did just that.

This woman squirted so hard, it was like we poured water in the middle of the bed. I had never seen her cum like that. From that point on, fucking her would always be a great experience. Listening to that gushy wet pussy splash as my pelvis banged against her ass and thighs. Riding dick could be a great experience for a man or woman, if the woman knows how to do it well. I love to have a woman ride me, especially if she has a nice size ass. Not too big and definitely not to small, but just enough to pam it as she sides that wet pussy up and down my dick. There is an art to riding dick because you don't want him to nut fast and you want to get yours as well. So you have to keep a rhythm going. Not too fast and not too slow, but a steady rhythm of both. Keeping that dick nice and wet so he won't go down but not too fast that he bust a nut quickly.

I was fucking this one girl and her rhythm was totally off. It's like she could go fast or slow, but her rhythm was so off that I had to suck those sexy titties when she was on top just to nut. I mean she was sexy as hell so no matter what position I had her in, I was going to nutt. This young lady could make the best fuck faces, I've ever seen. Those faces along with her moans could make any man nutt. This lady was so sexy that when I fucked her from the back, I always wanted to be by a mirror so I could see the faces she was making. Once I showed her how to ride my dick, the sex was off the chain. Every time we had sex, until she got it right, I would make her ride me until I nutted hard. I would tell her to sit on it slowly, then take it out and put it in again. Hold my dick and play with your pussy until it's soaking wet.

Sit all the way down on it and rock slowly.

Now start going up and down slowly, while pinching my nipples. Lean forward and bite my ear while you're still riding slowly. Once you bust a nut, then ride my dick like no tomorrow, until I bust a huge nut. When she got the hang of it, all she wanted to do was ride my dick. I know this might sound strange, but I had a woman train me on how to fuck doggie style. When we had sex, I was always turned the fuck on when she arched her back, when we did doggie style. This lady would hold the back of her legs and pull them close to her chest. All I could see was ass and pussy. That pink pussy hole was sitting right there and I pointed it hard every time. That shit was so exotic, especially when she would squirt from that position. It was like a water hose shooting water directly at me. That turned me on even more, so I would pound that pussy even harder.

One day, I asked her where she learned to arch her back like that. She was surprised and asked me, "don't every woman arch their back like that?" I told her absolutely not. Some women can't even take dick from the back. From that conversation, she would show me the different ways a woman could arch her back. She would also explain to me that when you hit the pussy from the back, the purpose is to go deep. That position is for you to get all of your dick inside the pussy. Of course, when you are on top, you can get your dick all the way in, but from the back, you can also put a thumb in her ass. Oh how I loved putting my whole thumb in her ass, while pounding that pussy. I remember when she stood up and bent over grabbing her knees, almost folded in half. She let me pound her so long and hard, while she squirted all over the floor. The way she would bend over and arch her back, I thought her spine was a rubber band.

That lady showed me so many positions from the back, I almost forgot about getting on top. I even showed this one young lady what she taught me about arching your back. It was like she was trying not to arch her back. Maybe because she always said I had a big dick and she knew I was going to go deep from the back. The funny thing is she had no problem doing it doggie style, but she wasn't going to arch that back at all. I kept telling her that I wasn't going too deep, nor was I going to hurt the pussy. SO she finally gave in and let me arch that back. I didn't hesitate arching that back fully, but I didn't go deep. The first couple times I put my dick in halfway, but not down to the balls. But one night we had been drinking and I was in total fuck mode. I arched that back and she was against the headboard, so there was no running. I had gotten her so wet from eating her pussy and other foreplay. That pussy was ready.

I went full balls in! No halfway or taking it slow. I went in pouncing away. She definitely wasn't moaning. She was screaming and I kept going because she didn't say stop. She squirted so many times, while grabbing the hell out of those sheets. I was so deep in her pussy and pounding her so hard, that after I nutted, she crawled up in a fetal position. Her legs were shaking and all down her legs were wet from her squirting. Needless to say, she never let me arch her back like that again. Honestly, I didn't care because I had accomplished my mission. I just wanted to wear her sexy little ass out in that position with her back arched. See, she had the perfect little ass, with the most beautiful chocolate skin. Every time I looked at that pink pussy, surrounded by all that sexy chocolate, made me want to go balls deep in her. It took time for her to let her guard down, but it was well worth the wait.

I don't like discussing this one young lady because she was even a little too freaky for me.

Everything was cool with her until she tried to do something I don't play about. We had just fucked really hard at this hotel. I mean, we did it all! Oral, fingering, doggie, missionary and more. So after laying there for a minute, she wanted to have sex again. She started kissing me, then went down to give me oral sex. She started sucking on my dick, licking it and playing with my balls. I was totally getting in the mood. My dick was rock hard and he was ready to play. All of a sudden I felt a finger try to go in my ass. I rolled over in a hurry. "What the fuck are you doing!" She so calmly said, "I was going to milk your prostate." Quickly, I said, "No You Weren't!" I grabbed my clothes and started getting dressed. She told me that so many other guys she had been with loved when she did that.

I didn't care what every other man liked, but wasn't no woman was putting her finger up my ass.

That was one thing I was not willing to be trained on. Like I said in the beginning, it's okay to teach and train someone to pleasure you sexually, if that person is willing to learn. That was just one thing I wasn't willing to learn. Sex is just like anything else in life, you never stop learning. When you think you know it all, someone comes along and shows you something different. I would have never thought a woman would try to put her finger in my ass! Then try and get me to go along with it, like it's just normal. Me and that young lady never hooked up again. Now I hooked up with a friend of hers, who taught me about felsite. She loved to have her toes sucked. I mean she couldn't cum unless I held her legs back, pounding her while sucking her toes. I must say, she had some beautiful feet, so me sucking on those toes was no problem. She would even want me to suck her toes, while watching TV. That not only got her horny, but when I saw how horny it was getting her....Damn! I got horny too and it was pussy pounding time.

THE BEAST WITHIN

Whether we know it or not, everyone has an inner sexual beast. This inner sexual beast is not released with everyone, but there are usually some people that come into your life and make you feel comfortable enough to release that beast. These in particular will make you feel like there is no judgment for anything you do. When you meet those people, you will know because something inside you won't hold back and you will let that freak in you come all the way out. Rather that sexual beast will come out. The reason I like using the word beast is because you will be doing and saying things that are not just freaky. The things you will be doing will be wild and beasty, with no holding back. From getting spanked, to being called a naughty bitch, or even letting yourself be filmed while having sex. When that sexual beast comes out, it's game on!

My sexual beast has come out with various women over my lifetime. I must admit that I was a late bloomer when it came to sex, but once I was not, I wanted to learn almost everything about sex with a woman. Because I was a late bloomer, it would take special women and I mean special women to make me release my inner sexual beast. The first time my inner sexual beast would be released would be

41

when I met one of my friend's cousins. I was in the military and she was an older woman. I had to be around nineteen years old. Now this woman was around twenty-eight, but she had a thing for young guys. Now I wasn't that experienced in sex and remember when your inner sexual beast is released, it takes someone making you feel comfortable, non-judgmental and they are willing to go wherever the journey takes y'all. See, letting that inner sexual beast out, you have to have someone on the same page.

I don't know what it was about me that made this woman feel that I would release my inner sexual beast with her. Maybe because I looked like a late bloomer and she felt she could get it out of me or I just looked like a late bloomer, and she felt she would get it out of me or I just looked like a horny kid. Whatever the case, she was about to make me do things I would never forget. It all started when he invited me over to his family house for a party. I will never forget it because I was stationed in North Carolina. This was my first time going to a party in the south. When I arrived, he introduced me to his entire family and I must say, those southern girls had some beautiful bodies. Every last one of them had on cut off jean shorts and those ass cheeks were hanging out. I'm not going to lie, even his mother had on those cut off jean shorts and yes, that ass was looking good. I didn't see not one ugly lady at the party.

When he introduced me to his cousin, I should have known something because she made a comment under her breath. She quietly said, "Um, some chocolate candy to play with." I ignored it because this was an older woman and why would she be interested in a young military kid. The music was playing. People were dancing, drinking and having a great time. The music slowed down and that's when everything took a turn. This cousin came and asked me to dance with her. Of course, I said yes. We started dancing but I was nervous as hell. This lady was built like a brick house. Ass was firm, tits were solid and round, not to add she was as fine as redbone. As we were dancing she whispered to me, don't be afraid to get close to me. I still kind of danced on her, I was definitely going to get an erection.

I guess it didn't matter to her because she took my hands and put them firmly under the cuff of her ass cheeks. Almost immediately my dick started to rise. I know she felt it because it was poking me in the stomach. Something was telling me that she wanted my dick to get hard so she could feel it against her. After that song, she led me by the hand to a secluded place, where we could talk. She asked for my phone number and we started hanging out. I must admit, from day one, she made me feel comfortable. I was so relaxed around her and I felt that I could tell her. This one particular weekend, she asked me to stay at her house. She picked me up at the military base, then we went out to dinner. After dinner and some drinks, we went back to her house. I had no clue what I was in for that evening.

Soon as we walked through the door, she went and poured both of us a drink. She told me to relax because I was hers for the weekend. Remember the thing about releasing that inner sexual beast, you have to be comfortable with the person. Believe me, she had made me totally comfortable with her. This lady took a shower and came out with a thong and nothing else on. I took a shower and when I got out, she was standing there. With no hesitation, she started sucking my dick. Not only did she suck my dick, but she bent me over and sucked my dick from the back. I was in a daze. She took me to the bedroom and grabbed this small dildo. She got on all fours, doggie style and told me to fuck her with the dildo. As I was about to put it in her pussy, she stopped me and told me to put it in her ass.

I lubed it up and slowly put it in her ass.

All I remember her saying is harder, fuck me asshole harder daddy. Like I said, she had made me feel so comfortable, I started working that dido in and out of her sexy red ass. The more I worked the pussy, the more she arched her back. I was enjoying her moaning as I wore that ass out with that toy., but that had nothing on what she was going to do next. When I thought it couldn't get any freakier, she laid on her back, put her legs back and told me to fuck her hard in the ass with the dildo. After I fucked her with that dildo, she told me to tie her legs back to the bedpost and fuck her pussy hard. I started putting my dick so deep in her that I felt the bottom of her stomach. When I was about to nutt, she said, "don't nutt in my pussy, put all that nutt in my mouth." I did just that! I nutted so hard, in her mouth and she swallowed it all.

That weekend, I think she sucked every drop of nut I had, out of my dick. We would spend that entire weekend with her letting me do all types of freaky things to her. I loved her being the first woman I released my inner sexual beast with. Now, she made me release my inner sexual beast with her, but it would be the woman that I help release their sexual beast. Like this young lady I met while I was grocery shopping, it was kind of funny how we met because she had a kid with her and the little boy was giving her all kinds of problems. I'm not a big fan of little boys disrespecting women or not listening. So I asked him why he was not listening to his mother and she let me know quickly that he wasn't her child. She said that she was babysitting for her auntie. After I spoke with him, he kind of calmed down. Well, he calmed down enough for her to finish shopping.

We exchanged numbers but to my surprise she would call me that very same day. Later that evening, I would get a call from her thanking me for how I dealt with that young man. Everything was kind of different with this situation from the beginning. First of all, I don't get in people's business, nor do I talk to women who are taller than me. There wasn't a huge difference in our height, about an inch or two but she was taller than me. I asked her on a date, but she respectfully declined. She explained that she is more of a homebody. She had been married before and her husband rarely took her out, so she became used to entertaining herself at home. For months all she wanted to do was talk on the phone for hours. This was something different for me because I was used to talking while I was on a date with a woman. I must admit that she was kind of nerdy or maybe just the loner type.

She wore those kinds of clothes that were not revealing, but you could tell she had a banging body under all that. SO one day she invited me over for brunch. When I arrived, I was impressed. Her apartment was not a reflection of how she dresses at all. Her apartment looked beautiful. Like straight out of a magazine. Again, I was totally impressed. Oh and she had on some jogging pants with a t-shirt. I was right. You could tell she was hiding that body under those other clothes. That ass was eating those jogging pants up. WOW! Those tits were big but they looked nice, small and firm. WE ate, sat around, talked, then I left. I didn't make a pass at her nor did I even try to kiss her. We both hugged and vowed to do it again. Once again, we would talk on the phone, but the conversations would get a little steamy. I would start telling her how good she looked in those jogging pants.

I would always tell her how good those jogging pants looked hugging her ass. I definitely couldn't tell her how I was staring at the perfect V print her pussy made in those jogging pants. When I talked to her, I could tell that she was getting horny because she would be totally quiet and I could hear her breathing heavily. I'm sure that pussy was wet. After about six months to a year, we finally crossed the line. When I say that I mean she finally gave me some pussy. Before she let me get between those legs, she made sure to tell me that she was not that experienced. She told me how her husband only had sex with her from the back or rather doggie style. If he did give her oral sex, it was just for a minute, so she never got to enjoy it. Little did she know, in my mind, I was planning on helping her release her inner sexual beast. Everything she had not done, I was about to take her on a sexual journey of her life time.

The first time we had sex, I was sure not to go overboard. I sucked those titties, bit on those nipples and oh yes, I sucked on that pussy. Her husband had to be stupid as hell because that pussy tasted just like pineapples. I licked all the pieces in and around her pussy. Just so she wouldn't be so thrown off, I turned her around and put my dick in doggy style. I didn't want to move too fast so I started off like her husband did. Oh but I did work the shit out of her pussy. By the fourth time we did it, she had started coming out of her shell. This time after I finished eating her pussy, she pulled me on top of her and put my dick in her pussy. She wanted it missionary! I put those long sexy red legs up and held them open, while pounding the shit out of her pussy. For her not to be experienced, she was definitely taking all the dick I was shoving in her guts.

After that, when we had sex we did every position we could. She rode my dick like a porn star, but that wasn't the freakiest thing she did. I mean this lady totally released her inner sexual beast. At one point when I would fuck her doggie style, she reached around and stated fingering her ass. That became a common thing for her. Sometimes after I nutted, she would lay over there, playing with her pussy and fingering her ass. I think she had several inner sexual beasts that she wanted to release.

Whatever the case, by the time we finished dating, she would not be staying in the house or not going out. She was a total different woman. That little nerdy woman was gone and now she was ready to enjoy this new woman she had become. I was happy for her because I know how it feels to finally be sexually free with someone who doesn't judge you. Sex is better when you are able to be free to express yourself with someone.

I'll never forget the time that I was dating this young lady who was in Corporate America. All I'm saying is she held a high position at her job. When I met her, it was due to her having issues with her husband. She was with her girlfriends at a restaurant for an after-hours cocktail. I was sitting across from them but she and I kept making eye contact. At the time, they decided to leave, she went to the restroom and of course, I followed. I introduced myself and told her how good she looked. She games me her number and told me she could not talk in front of her co-workers. I called her later that evening and she explained that she was married but going through issues. She was up front and said this could only be a sexual relationship. So clearly, she said all she wanted to do was fuck, release her frustration, and get her mind off her marriage. Now for her to be a white woman, she was built like a black woman.

I mean, she had ass, tits and was sexy as a motherfuck-er. When I say she knows exactly what she wants. I mean it! The first time we hooked up was after her company Christmas party. She asked me to meet her in a parking garage downtown. When I pulled up next to her car, she told me to get in. WE were in a secluded area, where no one could see us. She leaned over, kiss one and politely took my dick out then started sucking it. That woman them pulled up her dress, climbed on my dick and fucked the shit out of me. Our situation would last about four months but during that four months, we would both release our inner sexual beast. The last time we hooked up, she rented a hotel. A really nice one, I must admit. That day, we fucked in the shower, the bed, the bot tube and did every position known to man.

Did I mention she told me to video some of our sexual experiences from this day? She said that she trusted that I wouldn't show anyone.

When we left later that evening, she kissed me and said it was fun but I can't call her anymore. I simply told her that I understand. She said she couldn't risk losing everything because she was getting attached. I was a bit confused because I thought this was just sexual, but whatever the case, she kept my number. Months later, she did call and we hooked up again, releasing that inner beast on one another.

FORBIDDEN

Sometimes in sex there are things that are forbidden or rather things that people consider forbidden. Some people consider oral sex forbidden, but I think it's all up to you and your partner what is considered forbidden. Some people feel that nothing is forbidden as long as both people are satisfied.

My personal opinion is, if it doesn't offend the other person then it's fair game. I don't care what it is. If your partner is not offended with it, then do it! Now I'm a freak, but there are certain things, I'm just not willing to try. For example, like touching my asshole. I don't play that shit at all. I don't care how fine the woman is! Don't touch my asshole! Don't lick it, Don't rub it, just leave it alone! This one female friend of mine that I used to work with would always tell stories about how freaky her and her husband were.

One day we were working and she asked me, have I ever had my prostate milked. I quickly said hell no! She said that was something her husband loved for her to do. All I could say is wow! Then she asked me if my lady and I use toys. I told her my lady has a dildo that she uses if she gets horny and I'm not around or sometimes she would use it in front of me as foreplay. This lady told me that she has a dildo that she uses on her husband. What the fuck!!! I could not believe what she had just said. I told her to repeat that because I wanted to be clear about what I just heard. Then she said that she had a dildo that she uses on her husband. She told me that there are times that she fucks him first with a strap-on before he fucks her. The way she was explaining it to me was like he was totally enjoying it. The thing is she said it got her wet as hell, having him moan as she fucked him.

All I could say is whatever works for y'all. I know one thing: I never wanted to meet him after that. Not because I wouldn't get along with him or anything. I know myself! I would be looking him up and down, not casting judgment. My mind would just be trying to figure out how the fuck do you enjoy your wife fucking you with a dildo. Also, I did wonder how the fuck did that turn her on or get her wet by pounding a strap-on in her husband's ass. Like I said, no judgment if it doesn't offend either of you.

Then it's fair game! There are many times that friends or associates would tell me about sexual experiences they had that I would consider forbidden. But once again, no judgment on my part. One guy that I always played basketball with told me about the craziest thing that he liked his wife to do sexually. I totally considered that to be forbidden. We were talking about this female one day that was at the gym.

She wasn't playing basketball with us, but she was working out. While we were waiting to play another game because our team had lost. He leaned over to me and said that he would like for that woman to be him and his wife's next partner. Now this guy owned a catering business so I assumed he spoke to her and he was talking about something pertaining to his business. Man was I wrong! He was talking about her being their sexual partner in the bedroom. I was shocked! First, he would tell me something like that about his sex life. Secondly, that he would share his sexy ass wife with anyone.

Woman or man. He told me that he loved to watch his wife have sex with different partners. It didn't matter if they were women or men. He said it turned him on watching his wife get off with different sexual partners. This guy told me the harder a man fucked his wife, it made him even harder.

Not only did he like watching her, but he said his wife enjoyed watching him fuck other women. Hey, if that floats their boat, I'm happy for them. But I don't think I could enjoy some guy pounding my lady out in front of me and get horny. The first time I did something that most people would consider forbidden, would be with this young lady at the beach. She and I had been hanging out all day, just enjoying the nice summer day. As soon as the night came, we were not ready to go home. We pulled into the parking lot of the beach and sat there listening to music. We started kissing really hard while rubbing all over one another. Before we knew it, our pants were unbuttoned. She was stroking my dick and I was fingering the shit out of her. We let the seats back but it was hard to get out the steering column because at the point in my life, I drove a stick shift.

Every time I tried to climb over or she tried to climb over, it knocked the car in gear. Oh, but that didn't stop us! Remember I said it was a nice summer day and the evening was even better. At this point, we got out of the car and went for it. We took off every piece of clothing we had on. We fucked outside my car just like if we were in a house by ourselves. I mean we were so horny; we didn't give a fuck. I bent her over, I picked her up and we even put our clothes down to fuck doggie style. We were going at it for a while. The funny thing is after we finished, we took our time putting back on our clothes. That shit might be forbidden or some, but that shit was exotic as hell to me. Fucking out-side totally naked with that nice summer breeze on your ass. Rather the summer breeze all over your body. That was a hell of an experience and if I had the chance, I would do it again.

I feel doing things that other people consider forbidden makes your sex life more exciting. At some point, I would think that the same old missionary position would become dull or just doing it doggie style. Sometimes, you have to spice things up and be willing to cross that line. Try some new things. I know some young ladies your mother has told you that sucking dick is forbidden. Listen, if that's you, for-get about what your old school mother said. If you have a hard working husband that is taking care of business, suck his dick! Let that man come home from a hard day's work, take a hot shower and meet him with your lips around his dick. Suck that dick and stroke it like you are trying to win an Emmy. Your man may love to be inside your hot, juicy pussy, but sometimes, he would love to feel your wet mouth wrapped around his dick. While you stroke his dick, until he bust all over your hands.

If you haven't done it, trust me, try it. He just might like it and it may turn you on at how much he enjoys it. So many things people say are forbidden, are the very things they are doing to keep their relationships healthy. For ex-ample, so many women say that and sex is forbidden. Most women won't even try it, especially if you have a big dick. Now, I was never a fan of anal sex, but this one female that I dated loved me to fuck her in the ass. Sometimes, I think she likes it in her ass more than her pussy. Her reasoning was because her mom always said good girls don't do that or it's not ladylike. If her mother knew how much dick I was putting in her daughter's ass, I wonder would she still consider her a lady. The first time she asked me to fuck her in the ass, kind of shocked me because she was from a family of classy women who thought they were all that.

I can't lie, she was classy as hell, but slutty as hell in the bedroom. If I were a betting man, I'm sure her mom and sisters have had a dick in their ass before. The night she asked me to fuck her in the ass for the first time, we had just came from hanging with ere sisters. One of her sisters was celebrating a promotion on her job. When we got back to my apartment, it was the usual. We took showers, hit the bed and started to have sex. In the middle of me fucking her, she said, "Fuck me in the ass." I was tipsy, but I pulled my dick out her pussy and put on a fresh condom. She reached in her purse, pulled out some lube and rubbed it all on her asshole. She told me to go slow, but the way she was spreading that nice brown ass, that was going to be hard. I tried to put my tip in, but again, I don't have a small dick. Believe me, I'm not trying to boost, but it's true.

Statistics say anything over six inches is big. So if your dick is eight and a half inches long, and over two inches thick, then I think that's considered big. It didn't matter to her, she wanted me to fuck her in the ass. I tried several times to get the tip of my dick in her virgin asshole, but it wasn't working. Even my tip was too big. That night, she didn't get fucked in the ass, but I did finger the sit out of her virgin asshole. But that next night, she was still adamant about me fucking her in the ass. This time I lube up both my dick and her asshole. My dick was rock hard and I pushed the tip in her ass. She let out a scream so loud, I thought that I had killed her, but she didn't pull it out. All she said was wait. I let my tip sit in her asshole until she told me to go slow. I went slow, then she told me to pull it out because it hurt.

The way she screamed and how she said it hurt, I was sure it was the last time we would do anal. Not at all! She would keep trying until I was putting my entire dick in her asshole. Pounding it just like it was her pussy. It was like every time we had sex, from the point she wanted her asshole pounded. Even though anal sex was and never will be my thing, it was something about how she arched her back while holding her ass open for me to get in. I must say, she made me like anal sex with her. One of the most forbidden things to me is fucking a friend's significant other. Married or not, I feel that is totally forbidden and lines that shouldn't be crossed. While I was serving in the military, I would see this happen so many times. When guys would get deployed overseas, some of their good friends would be fucking their ladies.

This one guy would go so far as to be driving his friend's car while he was overseas. All along while fucking his lady. I always felt that he was playing a dangerous game. If this man ever found out it would be hell to pay. Thankfully I was transferred before he came back from overseas because I didn't want to see the fallout of that situation. I know this guy who his wife was fucking his step-sister behind his back. This entire situation was crazy to me because when he found out, he didn't break up with her. They all sat down and had a conversation. The end result is they all agreed to fuck each other. So, dude got the best of both worlds and didn't have to sneak around. Talk about a happy ending! He could have a different pussy each day or even a different pussy the same day. I'm not mad at him at all! It's not after two successful women would agree to this.

Workplace sex has always been and will always be forbidden. That's not to say that it doesn't happen but most people consider it forbidden. That's not to say that it doesn't happen, but most people consider it forbidden. In my opinion, workplace sex is forbidden, but it can be some exotic steamy sex.

Imagine sneaking off to a quiet office, where no one else is and all your co-workers are working but you are getting fucked good without anyone knowing. Then you come back to your desk like haven't anything happened. Everyone wonders why you are so happy or so sleepy depending on how much work you put in. I know, I've had some good workplace sex but this one story, I was told by this lady, would blow my mind. See, I never thought you could have workplace sex by yourself. She told me that she had a crush on our boss, but she knew he would never get with her because of how he loved his wife.

She would go to the employee restroom with her dildo and fuck herself, thinking about him. I guess there is an upside to her situation. She didn't have to worry about anyone telling on her or getting caught up in a workplace relationship. Having sex with family members is totally forbidden. Not only is it forbidden, but I will say it downright nasty. Wait a minute, there is a very grey area in this particular situation. My buddy had a cousin that really wasn't his cousin. Let me explain. This young lady was a cousin to him through marriage and she was supermodel fine. She was the complete package. This woman stayed in the gym keeping that perfect body together. So when he came to me and told me that she wanted to hook up with him, my advice to him was fuck the shit out of her! I told him to go balls deep in that pussy.

My thing was if the people in your family got divorced, y'all would not be related at all. Plus, there is not a blood connection between y'all at all. Tear that pussy up! Needless to say, he took my advice and got that pussy. Oh and just like I said, the family members got divorced. He kept fucking her and even had a baby by her. I know it seems strange, but remember they were only cousins by marriage. In my opinion, I don't think they did anything wrong. I know people see it as forbidden to have sex in your parents' house, but I must say, I did it. This one girl I was dating invited me over, while her parents weren't there. She sent her sister to the store and took me to the restroom to get what she wanted. She pulled those pants down and put that leg up so I could hit that pussy. Then let me get all that good pussy in her parents' house. Believe me, I didn't feel bad at all.

THE SEXUAL DROUGHT

Most people think of a drought as being without water, **but that's not what I mean at all.** When I talk about a drought, I'm referring to being without sex for a long time. I'm also talking about being without good, pleasing sex for a long time. I know it sounds strange, because when we think about sex, it's usually good or great thoughts. But let's be honest, there are some people that we can have bad sex with. Ladies, what about that guy whose dick is too little, he can't please you. When you ride his dick, it's so small that it keeps falling out. Think about that guy ladies who can't hold his nut and blows as soon as he puts his dick in your pussy. Those are just a few examples for ladies on how sex can be bad for them. Depending on how long you stay in a relationship with a person can feel like a sexual drought because you are not being satisfied.

Oh, there are women who can be the ones that's giving the bad sex. What about those women who are a lazy fuck and just want to lay there in one position? Think about that woman who never wants to try anything new. She won't do oral sex to you nor does she want oral sex done to her. Let's not forget about that one woman who never lets you get your dick all the way in. As I said before all these can be a drought because you are not being sexually satisfied. My situation is horrible because this one relationship I was in for fourteen years, my dick felt like it was on a deserted island. The times I would get my dick wet in this relationship would be so far apart from one another that I could strike a match on my dick, it was so dry. When I did get my dick wet, the sex was so boring that I didn't even nut. Believe me, I watched a lot of porn and masturbated regularly when I was in that relationship.

Being in a relationship where you are not being sexually satisfied can be totally frustrating. Imagine being horny as hell, then getting in bed with someone who can't even help you reach your climax. One night me and my fourteen-year drought lady had been drinking. We were both horny as hell! I mean we were so horny that I tore her panties off. My mind was thinking about getting in the pussy and how my dick was jumping. He was on the same page. I laid her down and started putting my dick in her pussy. The more I put my dick in, the more she closed her legs. WTF!! Here we go again. I'm ready and she is playing games with the pussy, not letting me get my dick wet. After a while, I stopped trying. I got up, went to the restroom and politely masturbated. My dick was too hard and throbbing, I had to bust a nut. I don't know if she did or not, but I wasn't going to sleep horny and drunk.

See, the funny thing is women are not the only ones who play games. Men can play the dick game also and put a woman into a sexual drought. I know this lady who had a live-in boyfriend, but he was constantly messing around with other women. She would tell me about all the times he would leave her at home, lonely and horny. Every time she told me these stories, all I could think about was fucking the shit out of her sexy red-bone ass. It was so hard for me to keep hearing her tell me about how he's not fucking her good. The more stories she told me, the more I thought about all the positions I would put her in. So one day, she told me about how he left her for the weekend and I told her all about how I could satisfy her. I told her how I would end her sexual drought. Instead of her laying at home thinking about getting that pussy pounded, she could come over to my house and let me please that pussy.

Of course, the weekend came and he did the same thing. Left her at home while he went out with his guys or hanging with another woman. That just happened to be the weekend she would call me and ask to come over. I said yes, immediately. When she came over, I knew she wanted some dick, but she was acting like she just wanted to talk. I knew what she wanted. That's why I had on shorts with no underwear on. It was impossible for her not to see my dick print in those shorts as soon as she walked through that door. She started talking about all the times he had left her at home alone as she sipped on some tequila. While she was talking and sipping all I could think about was taking those shorts and that tank top off her. Running my tongue up her legs right into that pink pussy. I just wanted to bite those nipples that were sticking out her tank top like silver dollars. Eventually, I sat close to her and started rubbing on her sexy ass legs. That prompted her to start rubbing on my dick. Oh yes, I knew she wanted me to take care of that pussy. I slowly unbuttoned her pants and put my hands in them to my surprise, she didn't have any panties on. I took those shorts off then sucked that pussy so good. I didn't stop there. I took off that tank top and lightly bit on those nipples. Her pussy was so wet, as I took off all of my clothes. Then I put my dick in her and put those legs all the way back. We were on the floor and I was fucking the shit out of her. I'm sure she wasn't thinking about how her man would leave her. I fucked her so long and hard, especially from the back, that she started seeing me every time her man would leave her alone.

It got to the point that she would come over to my house, even if her man didn't leave. I guess you can say the script flipped. Now he was the one with a sexual drought, not her. I'm sure the way I was fucking that pussy, she wasn't going home and fucking him. Every time I fucked her, I made it my point to put in a lot of work. I wanted her to have several orgasms and be so tired that she couldn't do anything with no one else. One thing I can't stand is to be in a relationship with someone who doesn't want to fulfill their obligation to sex. This is what causes a problem and in some cases cause a sexual drought. If you came in the relationship knowing that I like to fuck and like certain things during sex, then don't change! If you were sucking my dick on a regular basis before we got into a serious relationship, then don't stop!

Same thing for a man. If you were eating that pussy good while y'all were dating. Then don't stop once y'all get into a serious relationship. Do you really think a person is going to stay faithful if you stop doing the things you did to get them or go without sex? Women sometimes can stay faithful longer than men when they are going through a sexual drought. Men, we are built differently. That feeling of some wet host pussy going up and down on your rock hard dick is hard to resist. We may wait a month or two without fucking another woman or even masturbating, but eventually we need that wet hos pussy on our dick. Now I know sex is great for women also, but I'm just speaking from a man's perspective. We as men crave having that wet hot pussy on our dicks, as you moan to get that nutt out your pussy. That turns us the fuck on.

So many times I have been at fault for giving someone a sexual drought in their lives. I was dating this sexy ass woman who drove trucks for a living. She lived in my city but she was over the road a lot of the time. When she was in town, we made up for all the sex we were missing while she was on the road. I mean, we would have some of the best hard core pussy pounding sex. This lady loved being fucked hard. The hared I fucked her and slapped her ass would make her cum so hard. She was like a caramel complexion, so when I slapped her on the ass really hard, it left a handprint. That didn't matter to her at all. WE went on dates if she was going to be in town for a few weeks, but if not, it was all about fucking. It was about making that pussy happy while she was on the road. Now there were times I would get mad about something and when she was in town, I wouldn't fuck her.

I know that was wrong and there was a huge possibility that she would give the pussy to someone else. See, I come from a family of men who schooled us on how not to get caught up on pussy.

Also, I had women in my family who schooled us on how women think. The one thing they both taught us was, you don't control what's below someone's waist. In other words, a man doesn't control what a woman does with her pussy and a woman doesn't control what a man does with his dick. So if I played the dick game with her and she gave the pussy to someone else, it didn't bother me one bit. At one point in my life, I dated this young lady who was so humble, sexy, educated and of slender build. She didn't believe in messing around on her man. This young lady had all the qualities of a wife and more but at the time in my life, I was not looking for that nor was I ready for it.

My mind at that point in my life was more focused on enjoying my time in the Marine Corps. It was my second year serving when I met this young lady. I was young, freshly away from home and I had been schooled in sex but an older woman the previous year. It wasn't the time to be trying to settle down or give all this new found sex experience to one woman. There was one thing that I totally enjoyed about withholding sex from her. If I withheld sex from her, she would fuck me so wild when she did get that dick. I mean this slender sexy mother fucker knew how to work that pussy. Oh and she could talk dirty as hell while she was working that pussy. I went home on leave one time for a week and I didn't have sex with her before I left. To make things worse, when she called me while I was on leave, sometimes I wouldn't answer her calls.

It wasn't always because I was with another woman but because I knew she would think that and fuck me crazy when I got back. A week later, I returned to North Carolina and she picked me up from the airport. It was on a Friday, so I still had the weekend to chill before work on Monday. I told her to let me drop my stuff off at the barracks, then we could go get some food. Let's just say I never made it to my barracks. She took me straight to her apartment. There was no passion or anything. As soon as she opened the door, she took those stretch pants off and got completely naked. There was no playing around or anything. She pulled my pants down and started sucking the shit out of my dick. All she kept saying is I missed you being in my mouth. It's like she was talking directly to my dick. She was saying things like, go all the way down my throat because I missed you.

I still hadn't gotten all my clothes off before she sat me down in a chair and started riding my dick. Oh and did she ride it. I'm about two seconds, she was moaning loudly how she was cumming. She was moaning fucking me harder and telling me to stick my finger in her ass. I told you when she doesn't get the dick for a while, she goes crazy. I put her on that kitchen table, then put those legs back and pounded her pussy out. I loved when she got wild and freaky like that. My dick was so wet from all her nutt and that shit turned me on. When I was about to nutt, she told me to put it all on her tits. For her to be slender, she had some pretty nice sized tits. They were more than a handfull and you could definitely give her a good titty fuck. I nutted all over those tits. That lady was so freaky that she wiped the nut off her tits onto my dick and sucked it off.

That weekend we never left her apartment nor did we put on any clothes. Like I said before, I have been the one to withhold the sex, but I have also been the one who women withhold sex from me. One thing I hate is when a woman withholds the sex while you are in the middle of having sex. Now that's a different kind of sexual drought. Let me take a minute to explain. There was this one lady that I was totally into. She was bad beyond belief. This woman was so sexy and well-built that she was featured in a couple of magazines. I met her through a mutual friend but she and I never dated. It was just a sex thing with her because she thought I wasn't on her level. Actually it didn't matter to me because all I wanted to do is get some of that pussy. This woman knew I was into her heavily but she also knew I was the type of guy that wouldn't talk or put her business out there.

When we hooked up, she would play all types of pussy games. Like we would both get totally naked and she would have me eat her pussy repeatedly. She would nut several times and I would be ready with a rock hard dick. Ready to get some of that super wet pussy but she would deny me. Now that's a different type of sexual drought because the pussy is right there in your face, ready to go but she is playing games. It was more painful when she would get me rock hard then sit on my dick for a minute and get up before I could bust a nut. She was notorious for doing this to me, but she was all that and then some, so I accepted it.

I believe in the twenty time we hooked up, I might have fucked her five times and that's pushing it. Whatever the case may be, I enjoyed every minute I spent inside those legs. I don't care if it was eating her pussy or being teased. I truly enjoyed it.

UP AGAIN!!!

How many times in life does a man meet a woman that can make him bust that first nutt but get him up again and make him bust another one. I'm not speaking for most men, but usually when a man gets that first nut, it's a wrap for a few hours. Now if you're a woman that has those exceptional pussy, mouth, hand or whatever skills and can get that second nut out of him! Then you are in a class of your own. Fellas, if you are lucky enough to get a woman that can get that second nut out of you, keep her around. That means her skills are off the chart. Now ladies, don't get too cocky because there are some guys who can get that second nut all by themselves. Some guys have great dick control, especially when the pussy and oral sex is off the chain. It's like after he bust that first nut, that was a warm up. Now you're in for the fucking of your life because it takes time to build up that second nut.

So just know he's going to be pounding on that pussy good to get that second nut. Ladies, if you think that first nut was good, then the second one is going to have your pussy throbbing and your legs shaking. In my life, I have had several women that could make me get that second nutt but I have also had women that I would be the one to initiate the second nut. Fucking this one woman was nothing but fun because we were both so into one another that one nut was never enough. Talk about having some good pussy and being freaky. She was all that. This woman had the sexiest walk I had ever seen! When she walked her ass would swing from side to side slowly. It was like she was moving in slow motion. She was so sexy that she could put on a nice pair of gym shoes on some nice high heels and still turn heads when she walked into the room. This woman kept herself together from head to toe. Her voice was so soft and sexy, it turned me on.

Everything about this woman was great. When I would hook up with her before I did anything sexual. I would rub her naked body all over and just admire how sexy she was. This woman had my dick throbbing so hard that on several occasions I almost nutted just giving her a massage. Now if a woman is that sexy, you know you are going to get two nuts. I would live the way she would ride my face while she would be moaning about how she was cumming. Tasting that sweet pussy as she reached around and played with my dick while she was on my face. When I did eventually put my dick in her pussy, I would bust a nut so fast it was ridiculous. But like I said, that second nut would take some time. It surely didn't matter to her because she let me pound that pussy out. I mean she would hold those legs back and so side open that all my dick was going in her. I was pounding her out.

After that second nutt we would just lay there, rubbing on one another's private parts. She would be admiring how wet she got me and I would be admiring how wet I got her. I must say there was never a time when we didn't get two nuts when we fucked. Sometimes, when I think about getting a second nut during sex, I wonder if it's more fucking or making love, but I guess it's different with each person.

In my opinion, I would rather get a second nut during fucking rather them making love. The reason I say this is because when you make love, emotions are involved. Not that emotions aren't involved when you fuck someone but when you're making love, there are certain expectations that come along with it. When you're fucking, there might be expectations but there is usually an understanding between both individuals.

There was one woman that I messed around with and I know all she wanted to do is fuck but we always hung out together so one day I got confused. Rather I got more feelings involved that I actually should have. When we usually hooked up, it was at a hotel and we didn't spend the night. All the hanging out, chilling together, being around one another's friends got me in my feelings. I'm willing to admit that I was the one who took things out of content. See, she was clear about what she wanted. All she wanted was a male friend to hang out with from time to time. Then have some great sex with no strings attached, but I messed everything up when I tried to make love to her. I was holding her, kissing all over her, tongue kissing her and I did the one thing I should have never done. When I busted my second nutt, I whispered in her ear that I loved her. I knew I messed up because of the look on her face.

She never said anything about what I whispered in her ear, but from that point on, she became distant. As a man, I will admit that sometimes it's us that get our feelings involved. It's not always the woman. That would be the first and last time I would get confused with fucking and making love. Let's get back to talking about all the women who could make me get up again and get the second nut. This one young lady was so cocky because she knows that she could get that second nut out of me easily. Not only could she get that second nut out of me, she could get my dick hard anytime she wanted. This woman was a gym instructor so her body was off the charts. Nice, flat stomach, nice legs and arms, perfect ass, firm tits and her pussy print showed on everything she wore. One time we were in the mall and she grabbed my dick then started playing with it. Needless to say, I nutted in my pants.

Sometimes, I think it turned her on, making me nutt before I even stuck my dick in her pussy. The way she teased my dick was so sexy and seductive. I loved the way she would kiss me or just put her hands down my pants and play with my dick. All of that was great but it was just setting me up to fuck that awesome pussy. One thing about her is that pussy would be dripping wet when I put my dick inside her. Even if she didn't make me nut before we fucked. The pussy was so wet, tight, and tasty, but the best part was she knew how to work that muthafucker. She would make those pussy muscles grip around my dick like a glove. If you never had a woman grip your dick with her pussy muscles, then you are missing some real fun. The way she held my head while I was eating her pussy, slowly fucking my face. DAMN!!! That was hot! Moaning as she busted several nuts in my mouth.

Believe me, I licked up every drop of her pussy juices. In my opinion, she was a pro at fucking and definitely knew what to do with my big black dick. Sometimes when I would fuck women, just looking at how wet and shiny my dick was from the pussy turned me on. Me getting a second nut in these situations had nothing to do with the woman. Just hitting some wet pussy from the back, looking at my dick, going in and out of her pussy, while hearing that wet ass sound was a major turn on. I could nut twice easily. Same as if she was laying on her back with those legs back and wide open. Pounding that pussy as she gets wetter by every stroke. Trying to make her moan every time,

I pushed my dick in her stomach. If she moaned loudly or quietly, it didn't matter because I was turned on either way. I nutted twice every time in this situation, no matter who the woman was.

Sex is usually great but when you get that second nut, it makes the entire experience overwhelming. For women it's a little different because they can nut multiple times and a man won't even know. See it's not how many times you make a woman nut, but it's can you make her get that one soul snatching nut. That's the nut when she can't move after you finish fucking her. She just lays there with your nut all over her or in her. Her legs shaking, she lays in a fetal position or she's fast asleep. If you're getting that kind of result after you fuck her, then you have put in some work. You have left your dick print inside her pussy. With a fucking like that, even when you're not around her and she thinks about it. Her panties would get soak with her nut. Just the very sight of you will make her pussy wet and ready for another pounding. That's exactly how you want to leave that pussy.

So many times I put the dick down great and snatched a woman's soul. It is a great feeling for a man when she gets that first nut but you continue pounding that pussy until that one big nut comes out. That soul snatching nut! One thing about me is I hate when a woman brags about how good her pussy is or how she is always whipping it on men. I knew this young lady and that's all she did was brag about her pussy and how good it was. Now I must admit that some of the men she fucked with did act crazy after they got the pussy. This was a woman that I would have never messed with but I had to shut her mouth. I only knew her because she hung at the park when me and my guys played basketball. The way she talked I just had to snatch her soul one good time. It became a mission of mine to get those panties off her and show her how real dick feels.

I started complimenting her and boosting her ego every time I could. I went so far trying to get her that I even bought her lunch a few times. Like I said, she wasn't my type at all. She was a little chunky but not fat at all. Her body was put together well, but she didn't have any sex appeal. This woman was kind of on the goofy side. Now she wasn't ugly at all. A man would definitely take her out and not be ashamed to say that's his woman. She just wasn't the type of woman that I would go after. The day came for me to make my move. I invited her out and she agreed. We went to a free concert in the park then went out for cocktails. After that I took her home and we argued to see each other again. WE went on a few dates before I actually got the pussy. I was really having fun, just hanging out with her and I was talking myself into not snatching her soul.

Just as I was about to back off and not snatch her soul, this woman made a stupid comment, while we were talking on the phone. I guess someone kept calling on her other line, so she got irritated. She said so harshly that she wished the guy would stop calling trying to get some of her good pussy. She then politely said, I'm lucky she didn't give me any of her pussy because I would be doing the same thing. That was it. I made my mind up that I was going to snatch her soul. I was going all out. That next week, I invited her over to my house and she was definitely going to remember this fucking. Soon as she came through the door, I wasted no time letting her know what I wanted. I had on my boxers, with a tank top. When she came in, I smacked her on the ass and kissed her in the mouth. I had never done that before so I assumed she was a little surprised.

As she sat on the couch, I went over and sat right next to her. Like, I said, this was a mission to close her mouth. I leaned over and started kissing on her while I was taking off the little clothes I had on. I kissed her and rubbed my dick all on her, continually putting it in her hand so she could feel how big it was. My plan was working because she started taking her clothes off. When she took off these pants, I pushed her back and started sucking on that clit. I sucked that clit so gently, while licking in her pussy hole, until she was shaking and screaming, "I'm cumming." Don't think I stopped either. She literally had to push my head away because I had her nutting all over. When she pushed my head away, I thrusted my dick right in her pussy. I grabbed those chunky legs and pushed the back as far as they would go. I put every inch of my dick in her and pounded away.

I was fucking the shit out of her chunky ass. Just when I was about to nut, I pulled my dick out and shoved it in her mouth. I nutted so hard in her mouth and made sure she swallowed every bit of my nut. I knew she thought that was it and I was done, but not even close. I flipped her over and started pounding her doggy style. I was spanking that yellow ass so hard while I was fucking that pussy, I could see my hand prints on her ass. This was one time I wasn't going to put my thumb in a woman's ass. I put my middle finger deep into her asshole. I fucked her so long and hard until she screamed, "I can't take no more. Right then, I knew her soul had been snatched. This was only one of the times I would snatch her soul. After a while, I noticed her attitude changed. She wasn't bragging about her pussy being all that anymore.

Her conversation was more about how I fucked the shit out of her. It was about her trying to get me to be her man. In no way was that happening. What I did before I stopped seeing her is put this dick on her one final time. Her apartment caught on fire, so she stayed with one of her friends. All of her friends had those attitudes like she did before I snatched her soul. One day, she asked me to spend the night over her friend's house without her. Why would she do that? I was about to fuck her so good that it would leave an impression on her friend. Not only that, if I fucked her good, her friend would tell the other friends. Sure enough, I would pound that pussy out extra good. I would pound her out so good, her friend couldn't help but hear us. When I left that morning, I could hear her friend on the phone, whispering about me leaving. Well my mission was accomplished!

GOOD GUY / BAD GUY

In my life, I was always considered a good guy. I was that guy who always treated women nicely and made every woman feel special. No matter if she was fat, skinny, dark skinned, light skinned, black or white. If you were in my presence, I was going to make you feel special. Now of course, that did have some consequences behind it because some women would take my kindness the wrong way. She would assume that my compliments or flatting was me making an advance at them. This was so far from the truth. See, when I grew up, dark skinned men were not a thing or not considered attractive. As I got older, dark skinned men became a hot commodity. Dark skinned men started being seen as sex symbols all over, especially in Hollywood. If you were a dark skinned man, well groomed, dressed nice and smelled good, you were considered sexy as hell.

I always considered myself attractive but the era I grew up in, there were stereotypes of dark skinned men, but now that is over. I made it my point to treat any woman the way I was treated, by certain women, when I was growing up. It would be my soul purpose to make a woman feel special, no matter if we were dating or not. No matter if I was attractive to her or not. I was going to make her feel like a beauty queen. So being a good guy was someone I love being. As for being a bad guy, oh I truly love being a bad guy. I wasn't a bad guy doing bad things, but I was a bad guy in a good way. Kind of like eating a lot of sweets. You know it's not good for you in the long run, but you just can't resist that triple layer chocolate cake. Well, I was that chocolate cake with all the icing you wanted. I was the extra chocolatey cup of cocoa on a cold winter night that made you feel good inside and out.

See, behind closed doors, I was that freaky bad boy that made all your sexual fantasies come true. If we were sexually involved, all your freakiest desires were going to be fulfilled. I was that bad guy who wasn't afraid to try different things but I was also that bad guy who would bring the freak out of you. If you liked sucking dick, I was going to push the limit of your freakiness. Next thing you know; you were going to like swallowing my nut. If you were the type that liked to fuck a lot, then you were going to like seeing yourself on videos. I was going to film you, so you could watch yourself fucking when you were alone without me. Make you feel like you're still getting the dick. It was nothing for me to pull that freak out of a woman. For those that were already freaky, I was going to take you to porn star freaky. You were about to experience everything sexually known to man.

Sex toys, being videoed, spanked, and anal, the whole nine yards, there is no holds barred with this type of woman. She's the type of woman that's considered a bad girl and when those two cross each other's path, the sex is phenomenal!!! It's that kind of sex that wakes the neighbors up or has both of you taking the next day off work to recuperate. Being a bad boy definitely has its perks but there are downfalls that come with it also. One of the best perks of being a bad boy in the bedroom is, you don't have to ever ask for pussy, especially if you're putting the dick down right. If you fuck that pussy right and bring that freak out of her. You will never have to ask for the pussy again. She will be throwing it at you. Now on the downside, some women will lose their minds and become stalkers or overly possessive. They start to think that the dick actually belongs to them.

I mean like it's part of their body. As if they were born with your dick inside of them. That's why being a bad guy can be a good or bad thing. Oh and don't let them know the good guy side of you because now you are in deep trouble. Not only do they want to control the dick, but now they want to control your entire life. They want the full package. Trust me when this happens, it's going to be hard to let her go. You can't just wing her off the dick. You have to cut this type of woman off cold turkey. There is no nice way of letting her go. She has become mentally and physically connected to you. It may sound cruel, but that's just the way it has to happen with this type of woman. Eventually, she will move on especially if she is not getting the dick anymore. See the dick will continually cloud her judgment into believing there is hope for y'all to be together but if you cut the dick off, then she can think clearly.

That woman was truly a bad girl who had no problem showing it. The one thing I felt a little guilty about was when we hooked up and she squirted so bad that she went back to church with no panties on. Back then, I felt guilty but when I think about it now, it was kind of funny or actually freaky as hell. I loved women seeing me as a good guy, then getting them in the bed and putting all this and a half inch big black dick all in them. It was like a surprise to them once I got to pounding that pussy or sucking that pussy like a popsicle. It was a self-esteem booster to see them lying there with that look of surprise on their faces. I could just imagine the stories they would tell their friends.

One young lady told me she couldn't help but tell her cousin how big black and pretty my dick was. She told me that my dick was so good that she wanted me to fuck her cousin so they could compare stories of how good the dick was.

I was all in for that but it never happened. Don't think I didn't ask about it several times, but she never set it up. The best time I think my bad guy side worked was with one of my neighbors. I feel the reason it worked so well is because this woman thought I was a perfect good guy. She never saw a woman coming in or out of my apartment nor did she see a lot of guys hanging around. All she saw was me leaving for work and coming home by myself. Every day, I saw her, it was her and her child. There was no man anywhere around. WE never really spoke to one another except for in passing, but I do think she realized me looking at her a few times. When I would sit on my balcony and see her come home with her child, I would always make a point to speak. She was extremely sexy with long beautiful hair. Always dressed nicely and made that postal uniform look great.

Sometimes when I saw her, all I could think about was showing her my bad guy side. The day came when we would get the chance to have a conversation. We were both in the laundry room washing our clothes. All the dryers were being used and my clothes had just stopped washing. I was waiting for one of her dryers to stop and one did. She started taking her clothes out the dryer, then a sexy ass thong dropped on the floor. I didn't dare pick it up. That's when she looked at me and smiled, saying stop looking at my panties. If only she knew that I was thinking about how she would look taking those panties off. We both laughed and the conversation was on. We talked for a while, then she said she has to go fix dinner for her child. I surely got her phone number before she left. From that point, we would talk on the phone daily. I learned that her child's father was not in their lives and didn't want anything to do with her child. He had gotten married and moved on.

From the beginning, she made it clear that she wasn't looking for a father figure. Her family was all the support she needed for her child nor did she want to bring a man around her child. All she wanted was a friend who could satisfy her sexual needs. Someone she could hang out with on different occasions or just have a good conversation. The way she lifted me up as a good guy, made me feel good because being a single man, women always think you only wanted some pussy. I mean I did want the pussy, but at that point in my life, I only had one child and I would have been willing to take a chance with her. It was clear that she didn't want that so I wasn't going to push that issue. Now I did let her know that I didn't bring women around my daughter either. So I didn't have company at my apartment. If we hooked up, it would have to be at a hotel because we both didn't want people around our children.

Little did I know that she had a bad girl inside her. We would spend a lot of time on the phone or in the laundry room talking. The first time she let me kiss her was in the laundry room. Not only did I kiss her, but she let me put my hands down her pajamas and rub that soft ass. Things would get more and more heated every time we met in the laundry room. I remember it was a horrible winter day and they shut everything down for a few days. No one was working and everyone was stuck in the house. I was watching television and she called telling me to meet her in the laundry room. When I got in there, she had a cocktail in her hand and seemed kind of tipsy. She started hugging me, then tongue kissed me so good. I started putting my hands down her pants, rubbing her ass. She pulled away from me, turned off the lights and locked the laundry room door. Those pajama pants came off so quick and she bent over.

I put my dick in her and wore that ass out. I was fucking he so good, she took all her clothes off. Not me though, I was too nervous. That woman laid me down on top of her pajama pants, then rode the shit out of my dick. When I got ready to nut, she took her pajama top and wiped it all off my stomach.

After we finished, we both went back to our apartments. I took a hot shower, got something to eat and laid down. I dozed off but later that evening, my phone would ring. It was her asking me if I was ready for round two. This time, we locked the door and turned off the lights and we got totally naked. She brought a blanket with her this time so we really could fuck on the floor. This time, she sucked my dick before and after we finished. I must admit, fucking her in that warn laundry room was a massive turn on. Her bad girl side was equal to my bad guy side.

I loved it and enjoyed every minute we spent in that laundry room, until I moved out of my apartment. Sometimes, I wonder if those cameras in there recorded us. The maintenance person said they haven't worked in years, but if they did, whoever watched them got a hell of a show. I would fuck the shit out of her every time we met in that laundry room. If those walls could talk, the stories they would tell. I'm definitely glad I got to discover her bad girl side and I'm sure she's glad she got to discover my bad guy side. In my life, I have never been a big fan of people messing around on someone they are dating. Now that's not to say that I haven't done it, but I'm not a fan of it. The times that I have done it in my life, it was never me that pursued the person. It was them that pursued me, because they weren't happy in their relationship and I usually don't find out until I have already fucked the woman.

This next incident, I really didn't consider it cheating or messing around on someone. This was kind of unique because it was two women. I knew this woman but her sister was dating a female and also attractive to me. I would always joke with her older sister. If her younger sister liked me, I would be all over her. Well, to my surprise, her sister was planning on making a move on me. She was in a legit relationship. No matter if she was dating a woman, because love is love. No matter who you're dating. But again, it was me who made the advance on her, she made the advance on me. Sexy is an understatement for this woman. She had ass, tits, legs and more. The best part I, it hadn't been touched by dick or at least I assumed it hadn't, Well, she made her advance one day while we were all at a softball game. Her older sister played softball.

We were sitting on the bleachers and she came straight out with it. She told me that I know you be looking at me. Of course, I looked surprised. She went on to say how she's a woman and she knows I see all that ass. Why did she sat that because now the bad guy's thoughts were coming out of me? I told her not only do I notice that ass, but I think about getting some of that ass. Not being shy at all, she said "stop thinking about it and get some." I replied, "don't you have a woman"? But she immediately responded, " I do, but every now and then, I like a dick with a heartbeat. I enjoy the feeling of having a hard dick throbbing inside me until he bust a big nut." She said she loves to feel that satisfaction sometimes. So we set up a place to meet at and I must admit, she did not disappoint. I fucked her good and she fucked me even better. I think we both got all that satisfaction we desired from one another because that wouldn't be the last time we would hook up.

UNLEASH THE BEAST

By **this point in my life, I had been through a lot sexually.** From being molested by women, taught how to have sex by an older woman and being a late bloomer when it came to actually having sex. All that I had been through, and from even taking sex classes, so I could totally understand human sexual behavior, I considered myself a sexual beast. I had dick control, I knew how to use this big dick, I could eat pussy like a champ and I had experienced a lot sexually. I felt that there was not a pussy that I could not please. Within legal age, and of course, not a relative. I'm not a pervert; I'm just confident in my shit. I'm at that age where nothing surprises me about a woman with sex because there's always some experience in my past that relates to it. At this point in my life, I think it's the women that should be worried if they encounter this sexual beast.

I had gotten to the pint that I loved having sex like it was a sport. It was a thrill to see how good I could work a woman's pussy. It became my pleasure to please a woman. I know I would be the best at pleasing her. I looked at it as an art now. The beast that was unleashed wasn't a wild, uncontrollable beast, but a passionate beast that aimed to please. It wasn't about me getting a nut or anything like that. It was solely about pleasing whatever woman I chose to be with. Before you could ever get to this point, as a man or a woman, you have to master yourself inside and out. See, when a person has sex, they exchange bodily fluids, even if you use protection. Emotions can get involved and of course you are giving up a part of yourself physically. Not everyone will get to this point in life because some people are just happy being with one person. That's a good thing or actually a great thing.

The fewer people that you are sexually active with helps you to maintain your identity. You don't get caught up in trying to please several different people in several different ways. The thing about me unleashing my sexual beast is, I rarely unleashed it with women I wasn't in a re-lationship with, and if I did, I was the one controlling the sexual experience. Fucking this cashier, I had to really put my skills to work and totally control our sexual escapade. From the first time we had sex, I could tell she wanted to be in control. She would always start off riding me and try to dictated every position we would do and when we would do them. Hell no!!! I quickly took control of that pussy. By the third time, I fucked her, I unleashed the beast on her. I pounded her pussy in her garage, with her pants halfway down. Then I had her get on her knees and suck all the nutt out of my dick. I took total control.

I never stopped her from getting on top to start off, but you better believe that I controlled the rest of that sexual escapade. Like I said earlier, sex became a sport to me and I loved to practice in my spare time. I was never a fan of meeting new pussy, so I would always go back to women I had in the past. All the things that I learned along the way, I would do with them if I already hadn't. If I had then, we would take it to another level. Like the girl I lost my virgin-ity to in high school. When we ran back into one another, I was happy as hell. It was time to show her what this grown man dick could do. It was time to unleash the nest on her. Thrust me, I didn't take it easy on her pussy either. Every time I fucked her, I wanted her completely naked because she had a gorgeous body. I got so freaky with her that I totally surprised myself. What surprised me more than anything is she let me get outrageously freaky.

I had never used a butt plug before buts he let me use one on her. I freaked her out so bad that we fucked in a closet at her uncle house, while we were at his birthday party. Oh, yes, she got totally naked in that closet. I bet the way I was fucking her; she was thinking this ain't the same dick I got in high school. There was always one of my female friends form the past that was willing to fuck me. When I wasn't in a relationship, these women were the ones that would get the dick. Whichever one chose to call would be the one I would be fucking until I got into a relationship. Sometimes, not being in a relationship was the best sex I ever had because there was no attachment. Especially at his point in my life, because I must admit that I could make any sex good. My dick slinging skills were definitely off the chain. I could fuck the most boring woman in the world and make that pussy wet as hell.

This is exactly what I would do. I had a friend and that's exactly what she was, a friend. We could hang out together and never once think about having sex. She was a bookworm and always took a class in school. This was one of the things that I totally admire about her. See, I wasn't smart at all or rather book smart. I had common sense, but when it came to school, I just wasn't the type who wanted to sit down and study for hours. But this young lady inspired me to read more and attend school. Her mind was not the only thing that was attractive about her. That body she had was on point also. It wasn't like she had a supermodel body, but her body was put together well. She had an all-natural body. If she never went to the gym, her body would still be on point. Yes, her body was like that.

Once, we were hanging out and she had on a fitted dress, with some gym shoes. That dress fitted every curve of her body, from top to bottom. Her legs looked so sexy with that baby oil on them. Oh and she smelled so good, with that soft subtle perfume she was wearing. That day, I couldn't help but continually compliment her and her appearance. All I kept telling her is how great that dress was fitting her. She just smiled and kept saying thank you. It didn't help that we ate lunch and had some cocktails.

Those cocktails made us feel good. After a while, she started complimenting me on my appearance and how she loved how I treated her. She told me that IU was the best boyfriend that she ever had. It didn't make things better when she gave me a peck on the lips, softly. That peck with the cocktails, along with the compliments, sent a signal to my dick that this may be a fuck moment.

I wasn't thinking about this being my good friend. All I was thinking about is getting my dick wet. To a certain intent, I don't think that she was thinking about me bringing her friend either. We continued hanging out all day and as the day went on, we got touchy feely with one another. Those cocktails had me slapping and grabbing all on her ass. Not to mention she wasn't just giving me a peck anymore. She was fully kissing me in the mouth, tongue and all. On the ride back to her house, she held my hand while we listened to some slow jams. When we got back to her house, we didn't waste any time taking off our clothes. It was game on. I knew she was going to be kind of timid because she was such a good girl. It was time for me to take full control and I did just that. I started eating that pussy like it was my last dinner.

I sucked each one of her toes, individually and fingered her slowly. I was about to unleash all of my sexual skills on her. The way I ate her pussy, she had a huge wet spot on the bed and I hadn't put my dick in yet. Instead of me getting on top, I put her on top because I wanted to see what she was working with. In other words, I wanted to see what her sex skills were like. As I figured, she had no dick riding skills, but like I said, my skills were so good, I could make any pussy great. I let her ride for a minute then, I grabbed her ass while she was on top of me and I thrust my dick into her. She moaned so loud, I knew all this dick was in her stomach. I started thrusting my hips faster and harder as she moaned my name to the top of her lungs. At that point, it was like she sprung a leak. She squirted all over my dick at least three times and I didn't stop pounding that pussy.

I flipped her over in an aggressive sexy way, then put those legs all the way back. I held her legs back while holding the bottom of her feet. I put my dick in her slowly, but I put the entire dick in her pussy. I was going in and out slowly, but putting all my dick in every time. By the eighth stroke, I let loose and started pounding her pussy. Oh my goodness, how loud she was moaning and grabbing the sheets. This was getting me even hornier and I hadn't even hit it from the back yet. After I put her legs on my shoulder and worked that pussy, I flipped her over, had her arch that back, then hit that pussy doggy style. The way I was hitting that pussy from the back, looking at her sexy ass, I couldn't hold my nut. In only two minutes, doggies style, I was nutting all over her ass. Looking at that sexy ass, with those stretch marks and hearing her moan. Shid, I nutted hard.

To my surprise that wasn't the end. She asked me to spend the night and I did. We woke up in the middle of the night and had some pussy pounding sex again. Then that morning, we woke up and was at it again. For us to be friends for so long, then turn around and fuck the shit out of each other was wild. Well, all I can say is we enjoyed the hell out of that experience. I must say that the first time I ever got to unleash the beast was with a girl who stole my heart when we were younger. Faith would have it that we would encounter one another in our adult life. Let me set the stage for you. I was in high school and I had a crush on this cheerleader. Back then, she was fine as hell and extremely popular. We went to different schools, so I don't know what made me think that I had a chance with her. I mean, almost every guy wanted her. She was the shit.

I met her from seeing her in the neighborhood. We would always speak, but if she was with her friends, they would have an attitude if she spoke back to me. It was the fact that I wasn't a light skinned pretty boy. Nor was I a popular athlete like the guys that was trying to get with her. I remember her giving me her phone number. I would call her house, but they would always say she was busy. There was one time when she did answer so we talked briefly. I will never forget how she played me and broke my heart. I would buy her chips and stuff from the store, then we would stand around and talk. It's funny because at a young aged, you take that as someone liking you. SO one day, she told me that a group of them were going downtown to see a movie. She asked me to buy tickets for us.

I used the money from my paper route to get the tickets. I gave her the money because she said she could get good seats. The day came and I called her, but her family kept saying that she wasn't there. I even got one of my friends to walk over to her house with me to see if she was there. When I got there, no one answered the door. I called her for a week straight, then she eventually talked to me. She told me that she lost the money for the tickets. Later on, I would bump into her friends at the store and they would tell me the true story. They made fun that she took my money and treated another, light skinned football player to the movies. I was crushed and looked like a complete idiot. Not to mention, I was out of money. Well, things were different this time around. I had money, my own car, and my own place, with a lot of confidence. Not to mention, dark skinned men are a sex symbol now.

When we bumped into each other as adults, I hurried up and gave her my number. Oh she was still fine as hell, but with a much more mature cheerleader body. This time, I didn't have to call her first because she called me. See, like I said, I was in a much better position in my life. Sexy as hell, with money and full of confidence, I wasted no time hinting that I wanted to go on a date with her. You better know, she agreed. During the next few weeks, I would make reference to sex every time she called. I wanted it to be clear that I wanted some pussy from her. I didn't want to connect with her again or anything. I just wanted to fuck the living shit out of her and let it go. Now she didn't know that but she was about to find out. She agreed to spend the night with me at a sexy romantic hotel. The perfect place for me to unleash the beast on that pussy.

I wined her and dined her, then I pounded her pussy out. Honestly, I don't think we slept that night. She tried to but she was getting all this dick from past and present. I took out all my heartbreak on that pussy. I was fuckin her so good that at one point, I think she said I love you. Whatever the case may be, she got the shit fucked out of her. Check out was at noon. We had gotten out of the shower and were getting dressed. I looked at the clock, and it was eleven o'clock. I stood up, took all my clothes off again and fucked the shit out of her again. That last thirty minutes, I really worked that pussy. After that, I took her calls for a minute or rather a couple of days, but I eventually disappeared. Like I said, this was all about fucking and nothing else.

ABOUT THE AUTHOR

Keith "Kcam" Campbell started Kcamproductions in Chicago, IL with a mission dedicated to therapeutically assisting individuals to deal with the chaos of life through the performing arts. His films, books, and short skits will assist individuals with understanding that they are not alone while dealing with the chaos of life. Kcam uses several life experiences to relate to his audience through his work. Having overcome several chaotic obstacles in his life including a horrific divorce. The therapeutic release of seeing some of life's most chaotic experiences brought to life by his works in books, lyrics in a song, films or short skits can be life altering. This is exactly what Kcam does, with two published books *Separation for Elevation "Letting Go Chaos"*, a series entitled *Surviving Khaos* on WVTC network and several other projects to come. Keith "Kcam" Campbell is definitely focused on empowering and educating individuals on how to deal with chaos through the arts.